THE DESCRIPTORS HANDBOOK

mastering details in your writing

Mastering The Muse of Story

A young thief infiltrates a secluded mountain monastery...

Dense forests rife with danger and untold wonders

A locked vault symbolizes concealed treasures or damning evidence

Hostage situations are high stress settings where lives hang in the balance

Joseph A. Graham

MASTERING THE MUSE OF STORY

Library of Congress Cataloging-in-Publication Data

Names: Graham, Joseph A.
Title: The Descriptors Handbook: Mastering Details in Your Writing
Subtitle: Mastering the Muse of Story
Identifiers: LCCN 2023918669
ISBN 979-8-9892106-0-2 (Paperback)

Published By: North Poehls Arts, LLC.

Printed in the United States of America.

10 9 8 7 6 5 4 3 2 1

Table of Contents

Introduction

In the vast and enchanting world of storytelling, there exists a wellspring of imagination—a deep reservoir of inspiration waiting to be tapped into. This boundless source, often referred to as the Muse, is the driving force behind every captivating narrative ever written. Within its depths lie the seeds of countless stories, each ready to grow into a vibrant tale under the nurturing hands of a skilled storyteller.

As you open the doors to this book, you are about to embark on a unique journey through the rich landscape of creativity and storytelling. We will embark on a grand expedition to explore the mysteries of the Muse, and together, we'll learn how to unlock its extraordinary power to craft tales that enthrall and captivate.

But what is this Muse that we speak of? It is not a tangible entity, not something you can hold in your hand, but rather a metaphorical representation of the wellspring of creativity within each of us. The Muse embodies that mysterious force that whispers ideas, images, and emotions into our minds, fueling our innate desire to tell stories.

In the pursuit of storytelling mastery, one thing becomes abundantly clear: to craft stories that leave a lasting impact, it's crucial to establish a deep and lasting connection with this Muse. For it is here, within this ethereal realm of inspiration, that your storytelling journey truly begins.

Within the pages of this book, we will embark on a thrilling expedition through the rich and diverse tapestry of genres. Each chapter will transport you to a different literary landscape—whether it's the heart-pounding realms of Thriller, the spine-tingling horrors of Horror, the emotional rollercoaster of Young Adult (YA), the intricate puzzles of Crime, or the fantastical realms of Fantasy and beyond.

At the heart of each chapter lies a treasure trove of creativity: 100 story ideas, each waiting for your touch to bring it to life. These ideas are not mere abstract concepts; they are vivid sparks of imagination, ready to ignite your creative flame. They are the building blocks of your next epic narrative, your intriguing mystery, your heartwarming coming-of-age tale, or whatever your storytelling heart desires.

Consider these ideas as seeds, waiting to be planted in the fertile soil of your imagination. As you read through them, allow your mind to wander, to explore the myriad possibilities, and to weave them into narratives uniquely your own.

Ultimately, this book is your guide to nurturing your creative spark. It's about becoming a masterful storyteller, capable of cultivating and harvesting the ideas that emerge from your personal Muse and transforming them into stories that resonate with readers.

As we divee into each genre, you'll learn how to draw inspiration from a multitude of sources, from the ordinary to the extraordinary. You'll discover the secrets of infusing your tales with authenticity, emotion, and a dash of magic, captivating your audience and leaving them yearning for more.

So, are you ready to embark on this extraordinary creative journey? The Muse of Storytelling awaits you, and with each chapter, you'll draw closer to mastering the art of crafting compelling tales that leave an indelible mark on the world.

Let's dive in, and together, let's uncover the limitless potential of your storytelling Muse.

As always,
this is for the author
inside you...

Adventure

Epic Journeys, Limitless Discoveries

The Adventure genre is a literary realm teeming with excitement, exploration, and the thrill of the unknown. At its core, Adventure books transport readers to uncharted territories, both real and imaginary, where protagonists embark on daring journeys fraught with challenges, discoveries, and personal growth. This genre is fueled by the human spirit's innate curiosity and desire for escapades, making it an evergreen choice for readers seeking the adrenaline rush of the unknown.

The muse of Adventure is often found in the call of the wild, the allure of distant lands, or the promise of hidden treasures. It draws inspiration from history's great explorers, intrepid travelers, and those who have dared to venture beyond the boundaries of the known world. The genre often intertwines elements of courage, resourcefulness, and resilience as characters confront adversity head-on, forging unforgettable narratives that resonate with readers seeking the thrill of exploration and the satisfaction of overcoming challenges.

The target audience for Adventure books spans a broad spectrum, from young readers hungry for tales of youthful heroism to adults seeking to escape the confines of their everyday lives. Readers of Adventure expect to be whisked away on epic journeys filled with heart-pounding moments, unexpected twists, and the triumphant spirit of human determination. They crave the opportunity to explore uncharted landscapes, solve puzzles, and experience vicarious adventures through compelling characters. Ultimately, Adventure books serve as a vessel for readers to satiate their wanderlust and indulge in the exhilaration of the unknown from the comfort of their own armchairs.

Your Descriptors

1. Underwater Wrecks: Sunken ships hide valuable cargo.
2. Mysterious Caves: Dark caves hold secrets and unexpected encounters.
3. Wild Rapids: White-water rivers provide thrilling adventures.
4. Overgrown Temples: Abandoned temples are reclaimed by nature.
5. Treasure Maps: The quest for hidden treasure drives the adventure's plot.
6. Journey into the Past: Time travel takes characters to different eras.
7. Aerial Expeditions: Hot air balloons and airships offer a unique perspective.
8. Mysterious Labyrinths: Intricate mazes test characters' wits and resolve.
9. Hidden Villages: Remote communities hold untold stories.
10. Ancient Ruins: These hold clues to forgotten civilizations and secrets of the past.
11. Ancient Riddles: Cryptic puzzles hold the key to progress.
12. Lost Artifacts: Valuable items must be recovered.
13. Steep Waterfalls: Cliffs lead to dramatic drops and revelations.
14. Cliffside Villages: Coastal towns perched on cliffs offer breathtaking views.
15. Avalanche Escapes: Characters race against cascading snow.
16. Underground Labyrinths: Maze-like tunnels challenge characters.
17. Cursed Artifacts: Powerful objects often trigger adventurous quests.
18. Forgotten Civilizations: Ancient societies hold untold stories.
19. Mysterious Scrolls: Cryptic writings hold secrets and prophecies.
20. Underground Tombs: Buried tombs conceal secrets of the deceased.
21. Ancient Tomes: Cryptic texts hold the key to solving mysteries.
22. Mystical Islands: Magical islands are shrouded in enchantment.
23. Deserted Islands: Characters must fend for themselves in isolation.
24. Hidden Maps: Cryptic charts lead to undiscovered places.

25. Desert Oases: Small pockets of life in arid landscapes offer hope and respite.
26. Lighthouse Mysteries: Coastal beacons conceal enigmatic puzzles.
27. Underground Lakes: Hidden bodies of water provide unique obstacles.
28. Isolated Villages: Remote communities often harbor ancient traditions and mysteries.
29. Exotic Islands: Mysterious islands provide uncharted terrain for exploration and discovery.
30. Submerged Cities: Lost cities beneath the ocean hide untold treasures.
31. Archeological Digs: Excavations uncover buried secrets.
32. Pirate Ships: Confrontations on the high seas add an element of danger.
33. Avalanche Survival: Characters navigate treacherous snowslides.
34. Uncharted Rivers: Unknown waterways hold surprises.
35. Abandoned Mines: Subterranean tunnels are perfect for mystery and danger.
36. Lost Expeditions: Previous adventurers' quests yield new clues and challenges.
37. Exotic Bazaars: Marketplaces are hubs of intrigue and cultural immersion.
38. Petrified Forests: Ancient woods offer eerie landscapes.
39. Ancient Relics: Powerful artifacts are sought after by adventurers.
40. Underground Temples: Subterranean places of worship are both sacred and perilous.
41. Underwater Volcanoes: Submerged mountains create unique settings.
42. Lost Compasses: Navigational tools go astray, adding suspense.
43. Savage Wilderness: Untamed landscapes test characters' survival skills.
44. Tropical Waterways: Jungle rivers are pathways to adventure.
45. Mountain Ranges: Treacherous peaks offer challenging climbs and breathtaking vistas.
46. Uncharted Deserts: Vast sandy wastelands hold mysteries.
47. Arctic Bases: Research stations are isolated and treacherous.

48. Hidden Passages: Secret tunnels provide shortcuts and dramatic escapes.
49. Enchanted Forests: Magical forests harbor mythical creatures and wonders.
50. Swashbuckling Pirates: Rogues on the high seas bring action and intrigue.
51. Hidden Sanctuaries: Isolated refuges offer protection and mystery.
52. Underground Caverns: Subterranean worlds hide both peril and hidden treasures.
53. Underground Rivers: Subterranean waterways create mysterious settings.
54. Incan Ruins: Ancient sites in South America hold historical and mystical significance.
55. Volcanic Islands: Active volcanoes add an element of urgency and danger.
56. Secret Gardens: Hidden gardens hold beauty and mystery.
57. Steep Cliffs: Precipitous drops create dramatic scenes and challenges.
58. Remote Monasteries: Isolated spiritual retreats often hide ancient artifacts.
59. Expedition Camps: Remote camps offer shelter and mystery.
60. Remote Outposts: Isolated outposts can hold secrets and unexpected allies.
61. Wild West Frontier: Lawlessness and untamed landscapes make for thrilling adventures.
62. Volcano Expeditions: Characters face eruptions and molten challenges.
63. Jungle Expeditions: Dense forests are rife with danger and untold wonders.
64. Eerie Marshes: Swampy terrain conceals eerie creatures and hidden passages.
65. Jungle Waterfalls: Hidden falls offer both beauty and peril.
66. Dark Catacombs: Subterranean chambers conceal danger and intrigue.
67. Cursed Forests: Woods are plagued by supernatural phenomena.
68. Underwater Caves: Submerged caves hold both danger and hidden treasures.

69. Remote Islands: Isolated locales create opportunities for unexpected discoveries.
70. Mystical Mountains: Peaks hold ancient knowledge and mystic encounters.
71. Bamboo Forests: Labyrinths of bamboo conceal secrets.
72. Arctic Expeditions: Frozen landscapes challenge characters' survival skills.
73. Hidden Passageways: Secret routes provide shortcuts and surprises.
74. Tropical Paradises: Idyllic settings mask danger lurking beneath the surface.
75. Secret Waterfalls: Hidden cascades provide dramatic scenes.
76. Sunken Shipwrecks: Shipwrecks hold both danger and valuable relics.
77. Sahara Desert: Vast dunes challenge travelers and hide secrets.
78. Rooftop Chases: Pursuits on city rooftops create suspense.
79. Haunted Shipwrecks: Ghostly vessels add a supernatural element.
80. Snowy Peaks: Frigid heights present survival challenges.
81. Lost Expeditions: Previous adventurers' quests yield new clues.
82. Lost Wilderness: Unexplored wilderness beckons with mysteries.
83. Ancient Battlefields: Historical sites hint at forgotten conflicts.
84. Hidden Temples: Ancient temples conceal forgotten knowledge and traps.
85. Lost Cities: Forgotten urban landscapes conceal mysteries waiting to be unraveled.
86. Wildlife Encounters: Unique creatures provide both wonder and danger.
87. Haunted Forests: Spooky woodlands harbor eerie encounters.
88. Desert Landscapes: Vast deserts test characters' endurance and resourcefulness.
89. Mystical Pools: Enchanted waters hold secrets and healing properties.
90. Amazon Rainforest: This teeming ecosystem offers endless adventure possibilities.
91. Hidden Messages: Cryptic codes and messages drive the plot forward.

92. Vast Wilderness: Untamed landscapes provide ample space for exploration.
93. Tomb Raiders: The pursuit of ancient tombs leads to adventure and danger.
94. Haunted Mansions: Creepy abodes are perfect for solving mysteries.
95. Floating Islands: Airborne lands create surreal settings.
96. Mystic Caves: Magical caves harbor wonders and challenges.
97. Hidden Creatures: Mythical beasts add an element of fantasy.
98. Hidden Treasures: Valuable loot awaits discovery.
99. Uncharted Waters: Navigating unknown seas presents perilous adventures.
100. Remote Temples: Isolated spiritual sanctuaries hold wisdom.

Your Inspirations

1. A young thief infiltrates a secluded mountain monastery, seeking a legendary artifact guarded by mysterious monks.
2. A historian deciphers an encrypted message in an ancient manuscript, leading to a worldwide hunt for lost relics.
3. A solo explorer discovers an underground world inhabited by creatures thought to be extinct.
4. A reclusive artist discovers a hidden cavern filled with glowing crystals that grant extraordinary powers.
5. A team of geologists drilling in the Arctic unearths a frozen alien spaceship, awakening its dormant technology.
6. A group of adventurers sets out to climb the world's tallest mountain, facing deadly avalanches and oxygen-deprived challenges.
7. A group of friends embarks on a rafting trip through a remote canyon, only to discover it's inhabited by an ancient cult.
8. A scientist discovers a lost civilization living beneath the ice in Antarctica, dealing with ancient rivalries and mysteries.
9. A shipwreck survivor washes ashore on a deserted island and must adapt to the wild to survive.
10. A detective investigates a series of eerie happenings in a small coastal village, revealing a portal to another dimension.

11. A young boy discovers a magical amulet that transports him to a realm of mythical creatures and epic quests.
12. A team of researchers explores a sunken city beneath the ocean, encountering advanced technology and ancient mysteries.
13. A scientist discovers a hidden civilization living beneath the Antarctic ice, uncovering their advanced technology and mysteries.
14. A treasure hunter finds a cursed artifact that grants incredible powers but comes with a dark price.
15. An inventor creates a time machine but accidentally strands a group of people in the distant past, where they must survive and find a way home.
16. A veteran soldier is hired to lead an expedition into a war-torn country to recover a priceless artifact.
17. A scientist invents a time-traveling device, accidentally transporting a group of people to a prehistoric era.
18. A solo adventurer embarks on a journey to uncover the truth behind a legendary curse in a remote wilderness.
19. A survivalist is stranded in a remote wilderness with minimal supplies, testing their survival skills.
20. A group of spelunkers becomes trapped in a vast underground cave system, searching for an escape route.
21. A journalist investigates a series of unexplained disappearances in a remote forest, uncovering an ancient, powerful entity.
22. A journalist investigates a series of mysterious disappearances in a small coastal town, revealing a hidden cult.
23. An archaeologist uncovers an ancient civilization in Antarctica, triggering a race to protect its secrets from rival expeditions.
24. A solo explorer discovers a hidden cave system filled with bioluminescent creatures and unexpected dangers.
25. A reclusive inventor constructs a colossal airship to explore the uncharted skies, encountering floating islands and airborne creatures.
26. A botanist explores a remote island in search of a legendary plant with miraculous healing properties.
27. A detective investigates a series of mysterious incidents aboard a luxury cruise ship, uncovering a deadly plot.

28. A renowned climber attempts to conquer an uncharted mountain range, encountering legendary beings.
29. A journalist investigates a series of strange occurrences in a remote, fog-shrouded coastal town, revealing a portal to another dimension.
30. A detective chases a criminal mastermind through a labyrinthine network of underground tunnels beneath a bustling city.
31. A group of survivors must navigate a post-apocalyptic world filled with supernatural creatures.
32. A detective investigates a series of strange occurrences in a coastal village, uncovering a portal to a parallel world.
33. A family inherits an old mansion in the Scottish Highlands, uncovering a portal to a magical realm within its walls.
34. A survivor of a shipwreck must build a raft and navigate treacherous waters to find rescue.
35. A hiker lost in the wilderness stumbles upon a hidden tribe with unique customs and traditions.
36. A group of explorers discovers a portal to an alternate dimension hidden beneath a remote desert.
37. An adventurer explores a forgotten jungle temple, awakening guardians that protect its hidden treasures.
38. An archaeologist unearths a cursed artifact in Greece, triggering a chain of supernatural occurrences.
39. A group of travelers becomes stranded on a deserted island with unusual wildlife and secrets hidden beneath the surface.
40. An inventor creates a device that allows people to explore their dreams, uncovering hidden mysteries and dangers.
41. A stranded astronaut must survive on an alien planet while searching for a way back home.
42. A team of explorers embarks on a journey to the center of the Earth, discovering an ancient, thriving ecosystem.
43. A treasure map leads explorers into the heart of the Amazon rainforest, where they encounter a tribe with mystical abilities.
44. A treasure map leads a group of adventurers to a lost city in the Himalayas, where they must decipher ancient scripts to unlock its secrets.
45. A solo hiker becomes trapped in a hidden valley where prehistoric creatures still roam.

46. A group of teenagers stumbles upon an ancient map leading to a hidden pirate treasure, embarking on a high-stakes quest.
47. An astronaut on a solo mission to Mars encounters unexplained phenomena and potential alien life.
48. A group of strangers wakes up on a deserted island with no memory of how they got there, forcing them to work together to survive.
49. A young girl discovers an enchanted forest in her backyard, where mythical creatures seek her help to save their world.
50. An astronaut on a deep-space mission encounters a wormhole that transports them to an uncharted sector of the universe.
51. A seasoned pilot crash-lands in the Himalayas and must navigate treacherous terrain to find civilization.
52. A marine biologist stumbles upon an underwater city inhabited by a forgotten civilization.
53. An archaeologist unearths a cursed artifact in Egypt, triggering a series of supernatural events.
54. An adventurer stumbles upon a hidden valley inhabited by intelligent, talking animals.
55. A renowned climber attempts to conquer an unconquered mountain peak, facing extreme weather and supernatural obstacles.
56. A photographer captures evidence of extraterrestrial life during a solo expedition to a remote desert.
57. A marine biologist discovers a hidden underwater cave system teeming with undiscovered species and dangers.
58. A journalist investigates a series of inexplicable events occurring in a remote desert town, discovering a secret society.
59. A renowned climber attempts to conquer an uncharted mountain range, discovering it's inhabited by mythical creatures.
60. A team of explorers ventures into a hidden realm beneath the Earth's crust, discovering a subterranean society.
61. A detective follows a series of cryptic clues left behind by a legendary thief, leading to a hidden cache of treasures.
62. A photographer captures an unexplained phenomenon in a remote rainforest, drawing a team of researchers into a supernatural mystery.

63. A group of survivors must navigate a post-apocalyptic world filled with dangerous creatures and rival factions.
64. A treasure map leads a group of explorers into the heart of the Amazon rainforest, where they encounter a lost tribe with unique abilities.
65. An archaeologist discovers a forgotten civilization in the heart of the Amazon, complete with advanced technology and elaborate traps.
66. A pilot crash-lands in a dense jungle and must repair their plane to escape while dealing with hostile wildlife.
67. A group of friends embarks on a cross-country road trip, stumbling upon a conspiracy involving a secret government experiment.
68. A group of travelers becomes stranded on a deserted island inhabited by prehistoric creatures.
69. A wildlife biologist tracks a legendary, elusive creature deep in the wilderness, discovering it's more than just a myth.
70. An inventor creates a portal to parallel dimensions, unintentionally unleashing chaos as creatures from other worlds cross over.
71. A group of friends embarks on an expedition to explore a remote, uncharted island, encountering unknown creatures and ancient ruins.
72. A journalist investigates a series of bizarre phenomena occurring around the world, uncovering a global conspiracy.
73. A treasure hunter seeks a fabled gem hidden in the heart of the Bermuda Triangle, facing supernatural forces.
74. An ancient tree deep in a remote forest holds the key to rejuvenating a dying planet.
75. An adventurer explores a forgotten temple in the Amazon, awakening ancient guardians.
76. A pilot crash-lands in the Amazon rainforest and must find a way back to civilization while evading dangerous predators.
77. A journalist investigates a series of bizarre disappearances in a remote forest, discovering an ancient, powerful being.
78. A group of researchers embarks on an underwater expedition to study deep-sea creatures but encounters a lost underwater civilization.

79. An astronaut on a deep-space mission encounters a wormhole that transports them to an uncharted region of the universe.
80. A treasure map leads a group of adventurers to a lost city in the Sahara Desert, filled with traps and enigmas.
81. A young inventor builds a submarine capable of exploring the mysterious depths of the Mariana Trench, encountering unknown creatures and underwater civilizations.
82. A group of urban explorers stumbles upon a hidden network of tunnels beneath a bustling metropolis, uncovering a subterranean society with its own laws and secrets.
83. A historian deciphers an ancient journal detailing the legendary voyages of a lost civilization, leading to a quest to retrace their footsteps and discover their hidden treasures.
84. A pilot crash-lands in the heart of the African savannah and must navigate the wild while seeking rescue, all while bonding with a pack of lions.
85. A daring archaeologist discovers a hidden chamber within the Great Pyramid of Giza, containing advanced technology that could change the course of history.
86. A group of time-travelers embarks on a mission to rescue famous historical figures from various eras, facing paradoxes and unintended consequences.
87. A brilliant engineer constructs a floating city above the clouds, only to find that it harbors dark secrets and powerful adversaries.
88. A team of treasure hunters explores an underwater cave system in the Caribbean, encountering pirates' sunken loot and supernatural guardians.
89. An AI-controlled spaceship on a mission to colonize a distant planet goes rogue, forcing the crew to navigate the cosmos while battling their own creation.
90. An expedition to Antarctica uncovers an ancient alien artifact buried in the ice, awakening dormant extraterrestrial technology.
91. A group of stranded survivors on a remote island discovers a hidden civilization with advanced technology, forcing them to choose between revealing their existence or protecting the secret.
92. A geologist investigates a series of mysterious earthquakes in a remote desert region, leading to the discovery of a hidden underground world.

93. A daring escape artist is imprisoned in an elaborate underground labyrinth and must outwit traps and puzzles to regain freedom.
94. A botanist journeys into the heart of the Amazon rainforest, discovering a sentient, ancient tree that holds the power to heal or destroy.
95. A team of adventurers stumbles upon a forgotten underground city, inhabited by a society that has remained isolated for centuries.
96. A seasoned pilot crash-lands on an uncharted island in the Pacific, where prehistoric creatures and a secret research facility await.
97. A renowned climber attempts to conquer a colossal, unclimbed ice wall in the Arctic, discovering hidden ice caves and ancient mysteries.
98. A team of oceanographers explores the depths of the Atlantic Ocean, encountering mysterious bioluminescent creatures and underwater anomalies.
99. A group of friends embarks on a journey to reach the fabled "City of the Clouds," perched on a mountaintop hidden among the Himalayas.
100. An archaeologist uncovers a hidden civilization beneath the streets of Paris, leading to a race against time to preserve their ancient knowledge.

Comedy

Laugh-Out-Loud Escapades Await

The Comedy genre in literature is a delightful realm where humor reigns supreme. At its core, it's a genre designed to tickle the reader's funny bone, often through clever wordplay, witty banter, and amusing situations. Comedy explores the lighter side of life, inviting readers to laugh, chuckle, and occasionally ponder the quirks of human nature. It thrives on satire, irony, and absurdity, using humor as a tool to entertain, provoke thought, and provide a refreshing perspective on the world.

The muse of Comedy is a mischievous one, finding inspiration in the everyday situations and idiosyncrasies that make us human. From the comical misunderstandings in romantic entanglements to the humorous mishaps in social interactions, Comedy draws its material from the rich tapestry of human experience. It often plays with societal norms, offering a funhouse mirror reflection of reality. Authors in this genre are skilled jesters who wield words like jesters wielding jest, crafting scenarios that delight and surprise, while gently poking fun at the foibles of their characters and society.

The target audience for Comedy books spans a wide spectrum, from teenagers to adults, and even children's literature incorporates comedic elements. Readers of Comedy expect to be entertained, uplifted, and, most importantly, amused. Whether it's the slapstick humor of a classic farce, the biting satire of social commentary, or the witty banter between characters, Comedy books promise a joyful escape from the mundane. Readers anticipate laugh-out-loud moments, relatable characters, and a lighthearted exploration of the human condition that leaves them with a smile on their faces and a warm feeling in their hearts.

Your Descriptors

1. Deadpan Delivery: Characters maintain a serious demeanor while saying something absurd.
2. Political Satire: Lampooning political figures and institutions for comedic critique.
3. Awkward Superpowers: Characters grapple with bizarre or inconvenient abilities.
4. Talking Animals: Animals that can communicate with humans lead to comedic dialogues.
5. Astronomical Absurdities: Comedic scenarios set in outer space or on distant planets.
6. Exaggerated News Stories: Over-the-top news reports and headlines.
7. Incompetent Superheroes: Superheroes with unusual or absurd powers.
8. Culinary Catastrophes: Cooking disasters and kitchen chaos.
9. Physical Comedy: Actions and movements generate laughter, like slipping on a banana peel.
10. Comedic Monologues: Characters deliver humorous speeches or rants.
11. Exaggerated Stereotypes: Emphasizing common stereotypes for comedic effect.
12. Fictional Game Shows: Characters participating in outlandish game shows.
13. Whimsical Dialogue: Characters speak in poetic or absurd language.
14. Haunted Houses: Ghostly occurrences in hilariously haunted homes.
15. Bizarre Weather: Unpredictable or fantastical weather conditions create absurd scenarios.
16. Running Gags: Repeated humorous elements or phrases throughout the story.
17. Exaggerated Small-Town Life: Small towns with quirky characters and exaggerated charm.
18. Comic Foils: Pairs of characters with contrasting personalities create humorous interactions.

19. Time Travel Paradoxes: Comedic complications arise from time-travel mishaps.
20. Mixing Genres: Blending humor with other genres for surprising comedic effects.
21. Fish out of Water: Placing characters in unfamiliar settings leads to humorous culture clashes.
22. Time-Loop Shenanigans: Repeating the same events with humorous variations.
23. Wild Animals: Encounters with unpredictable or anthropomorphized creatures.
24. Mockumentary Style: Presenting a fictional story in a documentary format for humor.
25. Slapstick Comedy: Physical humor and pratfalls add hilarity and exaggeration to scenes.
26. Animal-Speak: Creatures with the ability to communicate with humans.
27. Double Entendre: Innocent words or phrases take on a suggestive or comical meaning.
28. Irony: Situational or dramatic irony creates amusing contrasts.
29. Pranks and Shenanigans: Characters play jokes on each other, often with unintended consequences.
30. Over-the-Top Antagonists: Villains with exaggerated traits create comedic tension.
31. Comic Timing: The pacing of humor and punchlines enhances comedic impact.
32. Time-Travel Tourism: Tourists visiting historical eras encounter amusing anachronisms.
33. Monster Mashups: Combining various legendary monsters for comedic chaos.
34. Competitive Neighbors: Neighbors engage in humorous rivalries.
35. Wordplay and Puns: Clever language use and puns offer quick-witted humor.
36. Disguises and Impersonations: Characters adopt comical personas for various reasons.
37. Social Media Mishaps: Humorous misunderstandings and misadventures in the digital age.

38. Absurd Situations: Characters find themselves in bizarre or ludicrous circumstances.
39. Magical Mischief: Mystical objects and spells causing uproarious situations.
40. Supermarket Shenanigans: Comedic scenarios in grocery stores or markets.
41. Clueless Celebrities: Famous individuals navigating everyday life with humor.
42. Parody: Mocking or imitating well-known people, places, or works for comedic effect.
43. Fantasy Sports: Unusual or fantastical sports in fictional worlds.
44. Fictional Sports: Inventive, outrageous sports and competitions.
45. Mismatched Couples: Odd couples in romantic or platonic relationships.
46. Innuendo: Subtle hints or suggestive language add humor through implication.
47. Holiday Hijinks: Humorous adventures during various holidays.
48. Sarcastic Dialogue: Characters use witty remarks to poke fun at each other or the situation, creating humor through irony.
49. Epic Failures: Characters repeatedly attempt tasks and fail spectacularly.
50. Magical Mishaps: Spellcasting gone wrong leads to hilarious consequences.
51. Pets with Attitude: Comically sassy or mischievous pets.
52. Superstitious Characters: Overly superstitious characters encounter comic misfortunes.
53. Alien Tourists: Extraterrestrial visitors explore Earth with amusing misunderstandings.
54. Reality TV Spoofs: Parodies of popular reality TV shows and their contestants.
55. Misunderstandings: Characters misinterpret each other's words or actions, leading to comedic confusion.
56. Exaggeration: Amplified emotions, reactions, or events create comedic effect.
57. Comic Relief Characters: Secondary characters provide humor amidst a serious plot.
58. Self-Deprecating Humor: Characters make fun of themselves, endearing them to readers.

59. Fish-out-of-Water Travel: Characters explore foreign cultures, leading to humorous misunderstandings.
60. Parental Embarrassment: Parents behaving in embarrassing ways in front of their children.
61. Embarrassing Family Reunions: Hilarious gatherings with eccentric relatives.
62. Dreamscape Comedy: Hilarious adventures in the world of dreams.
63. Double-Blind Date: Two sets of friends secretly set up a comedic blind date.
64. Alien Abductions: Extraterrestrial encounters result in absurd events.
65. Crime Capers: Inept criminals embark on comical heists or schemes.
66. Animal Outlaws: Animals behaving like human criminals in humorous capers.
67. Haunted Schools: Ghostly pranks and antics in educational institutions.
68. Psychic Abilities Gone Wrong: Characters with psychic powers create humorous chaos.
69. Cultural Clashes: Characters from different cultures collide, leading to comedic misunderstandings.
70. Failed Inventions: Characters invent absurd gadgets with unintended consequences.
71. Misguided Quests: Characters embark on absurd journeys or missions.
72. Conspiracy Theories: Characters stumble upon outrageous conspiracy theories.
73. Sports Mishaps: Hilarious incidents and blunders in athletic competitions.
74. Travel Mishaps: Hilarious incidents and setbacks during journeys.
75. Parenting Parodies: Exaggerated or unconventional parenting approaches.
76. Corporate Shenanigans: Absurd situations in the workplace, poking fun at office life.
77. Mismatched Roommates: Odd couples sharing living spaces, leading to comedic clashes.

78. Zany Sidekicks: Quirky companions add humor and contrast to the protagonist.
79. Eccentric Professors: Unconventional academics with peculiar theories.
80. Farce: High-energy, chaotic situations and mistaken identities drive humor.
81. Misplaced Objects: Characters hunt for lost or stolen items in absurd locations.
82. Accidental Fame: Characters unintentionally become celebrities in humorous ways.
83. Haunted Hotels: Comedic hauntings in quirky lodgings.
84. Animal Trials: Animals put on trial in humorous legal proceedings.
85. Comedic Duels: Characters engage in humorous duels or competitions.
86. Satirical Social Commentary: Comedy can highlight societal absurdities and inequalities through satire.
87. Comedic Tropes: Subverting or playing with common storytelling conventions.
88. Awkward Social Situations: Characters navigate cringe-inducing events.
89. Misguided Protégés: Eccentric mentors take on peculiar apprentices.
90. Unusual Festivals: Celebrations with bizarre traditions and customs.
91. Exaggerated Expressions: Characters display over-the-top reactions for comedic effect.
92. Fantasy Creature Encounters: Interactions with mythical beings, leading to comedic outcomes.
93. Amateur Detectives: Bumbling investigators stumble upon baffling cases.
94. Quirky Characters: Eccentric personalities with unusual habits or traits provide comedic contrast.
95. Botched Heists: Criminal plans go comically awry.
96. Hollywood Satire: Mocking the film industry and celebrity culture.
97. Comic Conventions: Parodies of fan conventions and geek culture.

98. Fantasy World Parody: Light-hearted takes on traditional fantasy worlds and tropes.
99. Cliché Subversion: Taking expected story elements and turning them on their heads for comedic surprise.
100. Inept Superheroes: Heroes with unusual powers navigate humorous challenges.

Your Inspirations

1. A misfit group of superheroes attempts to save the world while struggling with their bizarre powers.
2. A disgruntled mall Santa forms a league of holiday impersonators to take down the real Santa Claus.
3. A dysfunctional family competes in a reality TV show that promises a million-dollar prize.
4. A group of aspiring magicians discovers a spellbook filled with humorous and unpredictable spells.
5. A frustrated author discovers their writing has the power to alter reality, causing havoc in their stories.
6. A group of misfit roommates embark on a road trip in a sentient, quirky RV.
7. A group of amateur archaeologists stumbles upon a hidden society of time-traveling pranksters.
8. A talking dog becomes a motivational speaker, sharing humorous life lessons from a canine perspective.
9. A quirky librarian discovers a book that can bring fictional characters into the real world with comical results.
10. A time-traveling janitor must fix historical messes created by tourists with a penchant for mischief.
11. An archaeologist uncovers an ancient text that reveals the world's most absurd and bizarre historical events.
12. A rogue AI develops a sense of humor, causing technological havoc and comedic mishaps.
13. An ambitious chef opens a restaurant that serves dishes with unusual, unexpected ingredients.
14. A group of time-travelers accidentally alters history, resulting in humorous and absurd consequences.

15. A bumbling detective takes on a case involving a stolen rubber duck collection.
16. A group of bumbling pirates embarks on a quest to find a legendary treasure rumored to be absurdly elusive.
17. A group of retired superheroes opens a detective agency specializing in solving comical mysteries.
18. A struggling stand-up comedian's life becomes a sitcom when they move into an apartment building filled with eccentric neighbors.
19. A down-and-out musician forms a band with musical instruments that have unusual and chaotic abilities.
20. A small-town mayor declares every day a different absurd holiday, leading to hilarious town-wide celebrations.
21. A talking cat mentors a struggling writer, providing writing advice in the form of witty feline wisdom.
22. A group of retirees decides to become amateur paranormal investigators, tackling absurd supernatural cases.
23. An inventor creates a device that allows people to swap bodies temporarily, leading to comical mix-ups.
24. A janitor at a research facility accidentally activates a machine that swaps people's personalities.
25. An aspiring stand-up comic's jokes become reality, turning everyday life into a hilarious stage.
26. A group of inept bank robbers accidentally takes hostages at a comedy club during open mic night.
27. A young comedian discovers they have the power to make anything they say come true, leading to outrageous consequences.
28. A group of retirees forms a secret society dedicated to pranking the unsuspecting townspeople.
29. A group of misunderstood monsters embarks on a mission to prove they're not as scary as they seem.
30. A group of amateur sleuths investigates a town where everyone has been cursed with a hilarious affliction.
31. A down-on-their-luck musician joins a band of aliens who have a penchant for catchy, intergalactic tunes.
32. A group of amateur ghost hunters encounters a friendly, mischievous ghost who wants to help them solve mysteries.

33. An overconfident magician faces off against a skeptical scientist in a battle of wits and gags.
34. An ambitious entrepreneur opens a theme park featuring the world's weirdest attractions.
35. A pet detective solves absurd cases involving missing pets with unusual quirks.
36. A quirky detective investigates a series of crimes committed by famous fictional characters brought to life.
37. A conspiracy theorist stumbles upon a real government conspiracy, leading to ludicrous cover-ups.
38. An ordinary person wakes up one day with the ability to hear everyone's inner monologues, leading to comical chaos.
39. An app that predicts people's future comedic mishaps becomes a viral sensation, changing lives in hilarious ways.
40. An eccentric billionaire hosts a competition to find the world's weirdest talent, leading to absurd auditions.
41. An aspiring chef creates a food truck that serves unusual and wacky culinary experiments.
42. A talking houseplant becomes a life coach for its owner, offering quirky advice.
43. A group of strangers wake up in a bizarre, ever-changing hotel with a comedic twist.
44. In a town where everyone is a detective, an amateur sleuth sets out to solve the most trivial mysteries.
45. A down-on-their-luck actor discovers a magical script that brings scenes to life with hilarious results.
46. A hapless inventor creates a device that translates pets' thoughts, leading to hilarious revelations about their owners.
47. An aspiring comedian finds a mysterious microphone that grants them comedic superpowers.
48. A group of misfit superheroes forms a support group to cope with their bizarre powers and personal problems.
49. A group of unlikely friends opens a detective agency specializing in solving supernatural mysteries.
50. A group of unlikely allies forms a support group for those who have survived bizarre, near-death experiences.
51. A small-town diner becomes a hot spot for supernatural creatures looking for a good meal.

52. A fashion designer creates a line of clothing based on bizarre and impractical concepts.
53. A group of conspiracy theorists stumbles upon a real conspiracy involving extraterrestrial stand-up comedians.
54. A group of amateur explorers discovers a hidden island inhabited by talking animals with unusual demands.
55. A clumsy time traveler accidentally lands in famous historical events, causing comedic chaos.
56. A misfit group of circus performers decides to go on a world tour, showcasing their unusual talents.
57. A misanthropic scientist invents a device that forces people to speak only in rhymes.
58. A struggling artist discovers that their paintings can predict absurd future events.
59. A group of eccentric treasure hunters embarks on a quest to find a legendary, nonsensical treasure.
60. A barista's life turns topsy-turvy when they discover the coffee shop's espresso machine has a magical secret.
61. A radio DJ stumbles upon a mysterious frequency that broadcasts absurd and humorous messages from the future.
62. A disgruntled puppeteer discovers that their puppets have a mind of their own and a penchant for mischief.
63. An overenthusiastic wedding planner attempts to organize the zaniest wedding ever.
64. A group of friends starts a paranormal pest control service, ridding homes of mischievous supernatural creatures.
65. A quirky inventor creates a device that allows people to swap personalities temporarily, leading to humorous mix-ups.
66. A chaotic circus troupe's misadventures lead to laughter and camaraderie under the big top.
67. An eccentric inventor creates a machine that brings fictional characters to life, leading to comedic chaos.
68. A group of retirees forms a roller derby team, defying stereotypes and causing comedic mayhem on the rink.
69. A librarian accidentally awakens the characters from classic novels, leading to literary chaos.
70. A time-traveling tour guide leads tourists on a journey through history's most absurd moments.

71. An accidental time traveler gets stuck in the past, accidentally altering history with humorous consequences.
72. A time-traveling stand-up comedian inadvertently becomes a court jester in medieval times.
73. An enchanted antique store contains items that bring chaos and hilarity to those who possess them.
74. A restaurant critic with a refined palate is transported to a dimension of absurd culinary delights.
75. A talking parrot reveals a family's deepest secrets, causing uproarious family reunions.
76. In a world where people have random superpowers, a character grapples with the most useless ability imaginable.
77. A professional clown decides to become a vigilante, fighting crime with slapstick antics.
78. A fast-food employee discovers a magical sauce that grants bizarre wishes to customers.
79. A mysterious cereal box prize grants unusual and unpredictable superpowers to those who find it.
80. Two rival food trucks engage in an escalating prank war, leaving customers in stitches.
81. A time-traveling detective agency specializes in solving crimes across different historical eras.
82. A group of misfit adventurers embarks on a quest to find a mythical creature with an absurdly long name.
83. An unlucky lottery winner embarks on a series of extravagant misadventures.
84. A disgruntled telemarketer discovers a magical phone that grants absurd wishes to anyone they call.
85. A group of friends opens a detective agency specializing in solving crimes involving absurd conspiracies.
86. A time-traveling delivery service caters to customers' requests for items from different time periods, leading to hilarious mix-ups.
87. A reclusive inventor creates a device that brings inanimate objects to life, leading to comedic chaos in their workshop.
88. A group of quirky neighbors forms a band to compete in a "Battle of the Bands" contest.

89. A struggling stand-up comedian starts receiving joke suggestions from an otherworldly source with hilarious results.
90. A town's annual festival goes awry when a series of bizarre coincidences and pranks occur.
91. An amnesiac alien crash-lands on Earth and inadvertently becomes a famous comedian.
92. A clumsy detective stumbles upon a series of crimes committed by notorious celebrity impersonators.
93. A group of competitive parents forms a chaotic youth soccer league with no rules.
94. A group of amateur filmmakers accidentally captures footage of real supernatural events while making a mockumentary.
95. A disgruntled theme park mascot decides to wreak havoc on the park's attractions.
96. An AI dating app pairs users with the most incompatible partners, leading to comedic romantic disasters.
97. A small-town mayor's office is taken over by a committee of sassy senior citizens with humorous agendas.
98. A struggling comedian gets a job as a tour guide at a haunted mansion, only to discover the ghosts have a sense of humor.
99. An overzealous gardener discovers a rare plant that has a taste for pranks and mischief.
100. A quirky family moves into a haunted house and decides to coexist with the comical ghosts.

3

Crime

Solving Mysteries, Pursuing Justice

The Crime genre in literature stands as a compelling exploration of the human capacity for both virtue and vice, with a distinct focus on the darker facets of humanity. It immerses readers in a realm of criminal activities, intricate investigations, and the intricate motivations that propel characters to commit unlawful deeds. Within the pages of Crime novels, one finds a multifaceted landscape where the scales of justice teeter precariously, and the pursuit of truth evolves into a riveting odyssey replete with suspense, moral dilemmas, and psychological intricacies.

This genre draws its inspiration from a myriad of sources, including real-life criminal cases, historical mysteries, and the profound allure of human behavior. Authors in the Crime genre are often intrigued by the complex interplay of motives that underlie criminal acts, exploring the labyrinthine psychology of both criminals and those dedicated to solving their misdeeds. The relationship between this genre and its muse is symbiotic, as it channels the multifarious nature of human morality and transgression into narratives that captivate readers.

The target audience for Crime books encompasses a diverse spectrum of readers. Mystery enthusiasts, thrill-seekers, and those fascinated by the intricacies of justice are naturally drawn to this genre. Readers of Crime fiction anticipate engaging with intricate plots, employing their deductive skills as they attempt to decipher mysteries alongside the characters, and immersing themselves in an atmosphere of tension, suspense, and moral ambiguity. They seek narratives that dive into the shadowy realms of human behavior, where motives are as enigmatic as the crimes themselves, and where justice, though often delayed, ultimately prevails. In essence, Crime fiction continually enthralls and challenges its audience with its gripping exploration of the human psyche and the relentless pursuit of truth.

Your Descriptors

1. Gritty Urban Landscapes: These settings create a stark backdrop for criminal activities, highlighting the contrast between the city's dark underbelly and its more polished facade.
2. Small-Town Secrets: In tight-knit communities, these secrets fester, serving as a catalyst for suspense and intrigue.
3. Forensic Laboratories: These settings provide a scientific angle to crime-solving, emphasizing the role of technology and evidence in investigations.
4. Seedy Bars: Often frequented by criminals and informants, they serve as hubs for shady dealings and gathering crucial information.
5. Prisons and Penitentiaries: They offer insights into the criminal mindset and often serve as settings for confrontations or escapes.
6. Detective Agencies: These establishments are central to many crime narratives, featuring skilled investigators tackling cases of all kinds.
7. Mysterious Islands: Isolated islands add an element of isolation and suspense, making them ideal for stories involving unsolved mysteries or hidden crimes.
8. Dilapidated Warehouses: These abandoned structures create atmospheric settings for criminal rendezvous, showdowns, or illicit activities.
9. Noir Atmosphere: The dark, moody ambiance of noir settings adds a sense of danger and moral ambiguity to the narrative.
10. Undercover Operations: These settings explore the complexities of deception, trust, and betrayal within law enforcement agencies.
11. Illegal Casinos: These venues often feature in stories involving gambling, organized crime, and high-stakes heists.
12. Rural Backroads: These settings create a sense of isolation and danger, often used for crimes like kidnappings or clandestine meetings.
13. Abandoned Factories: They offer eerie settings for criminal activities, making them suitable for stories with a haunting or suspenseful tone.

14. Foggy Streets: Fog adds an element of uncertainty and concealment, creating an ideal backdrop for mysterious crimes.
15. Subway Stations: These settings offer opportunities for chase scenes, tense encounters, and hidden threats.
16. Interrogation Rooms: They are pivotal settings for confrontations between law enforcement and suspects, often revealing critical information.
17. Historic Mansions: These opulent settings contrast with criminal activities, emphasizing the clash between wealth and illicit behavior.
18. Witness Protection Programs: These settings explore the lives of individuals forced to adopt new identities to escape criminal threats.
19. Political Corruption: This theme highlights the manipulation of power and the moral dilemmas faced by those seeking justice.
20. Gang Hideouts: These settings showcase criminal organizations' inner workings and the challenges of infiltrating them.
21. Underground Fight Clubs: They often feature in stories involving illegal activities, crime lords, and hidden agendas.
22. Clandestine Meetings in Cafés: These settings create an atmosphere of secrecy and intrigue, ideal for plotting or covert operations.
23. Chase Scenes in Rooftops: Rooftop settings add tension and danger to pursuit sequences, with characters navigating heights and obstacles.
24. Law Offices: These settings can involve legal thrillers, highlighting courtroom drama and ethical dilemmas.
25. Family Mansions: The juxtaposition of wealth and family secrets can lead to intriguing narratives in crime stories.
26. Beach Resorts: These settings provide opportunities for criminal activities in luxurious surroundings, often involving fraud or blackmail.
27. Abandoned Asylums: Their eerie atmosphere adds a psychological dimension to crime narratives, exploring madness and hidden traumas.
28. Amusement Parks: These settings create a sense of nostalgia and innocence, making them ideal for crimes that disrupt the fun.

29. Crime Scenes: These are central to crime novels, serving as the starting point for investigations and revealing crucial clues.
30. Suburban Neighborhoods: The facade of normalcy in these settings contrasts with the crimes hidden beneath the surface.
31. Drug Cartel Strongholds: These settings emphasize the dangerous and high-stakes world of drug trafficking and organized crime.
32. Cold Cases: Unsolved mysteries from the past offer opportunities for investigators to revisit old evidence and uncover new leads.
33. Pawnshops: These settings feature in stories involving stolen goods, shady deals, and desperate characters.
34. Hostage Situations: High-stress settings where lives hang in the balance, often involving negotiations and strategic planning.
35. Police Precincts: The bureaucratic and procedural aspects of law enforcement play a significant role in crime narratives.
36. Crime Scene Photos: Visual documentation of crime scenes can provide essential clues and serve as a storytelling device.
37. Underground Tunnels: These settings create a sense of claustrophobia and danger, often used for escapes or covert operations.
38. Criminal Courtrooms: These settings emphasize legal drama, courtroom confrontations, and the pursuit of justice.
39. Mysterious Island Retreats: Remote islands serve as settings for secretive gatherings, hidden motives, and unsolved mysteries.
40. Blackmail Letters: These plot devices often drive characters to desperate actions, leading to suspenseful narratives.
41. Morgues: Settings where autopsies are performed, offering forensic insights into the cause of death.
42. Psychiatric Hospitals: These settings dive into the minds of criminals, exploring the intersection of mental illness and criminal behavior.
43. Undercover Safehouses: These hidden locations provide shelter for characters in danger, often used by spies or informants.
44. Bustling Train Stations: The chaos and anonymity of train stations can be used for criminal activities, escapes, or encounters.

45. Shady Informant Meetings: Settings where informants provide valuable but risky information, often fraught with danger.
46. Illegal Drug Labs: These settings explore the production and distribution of narcotics, often leading to confrontations.
47. Prison Yard Brawls: Violent confrontations in prison settings, showcasing power struggles among inmates.
48. Organized Crime Meetings: These settings bring together crime bosses, henchmen, and rival gangs, creating opportunities for intrigue and conflict.
49. Shady Antique Shops: These shops often feature stolen or valuable items, leading to investigations and confrontations.
50. Criminal Safe Deposit Boxes: Hidden compartments where criminals stash incriminating evidence or stolen goods.
51. Cemetery Discoveries: Settings involving gravesites or mausoleums, often tied to unsolved murders or buried secrets.
52. Hidden Microphones: Surveillance devices that reveal secretive conversations, driving investigations and paranoia.
53. Stolen Art Galleries: Settings where stolen artworks are bought and sold on the black market, often leading to heists.
54. Dive Bars: Seedy bars frequented by criminals, providing opportunities for encounters, deals, and disputes.
55. Hotel Room Surveillance: Settings featuring covert monitoring of suspects, often revealing unexpected revelations.
56. Wiretapped Conversations: Transcripts of recorded conversations used as evidence in investigations or trials.
57. Undercover Heists: Criminal schemes that involve infiltrating secure locations, often with intricate planning and high stakes.
58. Criminal Confession Rooms: Settings where suspects are questioned and may reveal incriminating information.
59. Witness Stand Testimonies: Legal settings where witnesses provide crucial information during trials.
60. Undercover Nightclubs: Nightclubs where characters gather information, make contacts, or engage in criminal activities.
61. Smuggler's Docks: These settings involve the covert transportation of contraband goods, often leading to confrontations.
62. Hidden Chambers: Secret rooms or compartments where criminals hide evidence or escape capture.

63. Interstate Truck Stops: Settings involving long-haul truckers, often used for illegal activities like smuggling.
64. Undercover Drug Buys: High-risk settings where law enforcement officers pose as buyers to apprehend drug dealers.
65. Criminal Getaways: Locations where criminals plan their escape routes and evade capture.
66. Illegal Fight Rings: Underground arenas where characters engage in brutal fights, often for profit or entertainment.
67. Stolen Identities: These plot devices involve characters assuming false identities, leading to identity theft and deception.
68. Undercover Surveillance Vans: These vehicles are used to monitor suspects discreetly, often with advanced technology.
69. Counterfeit Currency Operations: Settings where counterfeit money is produced, leading to financial crimes.
70. Pawned Stolen Goods: Pawnshops that unknowingly accept stolen items, leading to investigations.
71. Witness Protection Safehouses: Locations where witnesses are hidden and protected from criminals seeking retribution.
72. Hidden Tunnels: Secret passageways that characters use for escapes, smuggling, or covert operations.
73. Undercover Casinos: These venues often feature illegal gambling and criminal activities, posing risks for characters.
74. Hijacked Airplanes: Settings involving plane hijackings, often leading to intense confrontations and negotiations.
75. Mysterious Cryptic Messages: Clues or messages left by criminals, creating puzzles for investigators to decipher.
76. Criminal Handoffs: Locations where illegal goods or information are exchanged between parties.
77. Witness Abduction Hideouts: Settings where witnesses are held captive by criminals seeking to prevent their testimony.
78. Illicit Auction Houses: These venues feature the sale of stolen or illegal items, often attracting crime syndicates.
79. Undercover Wire Transfers: Financial transactions used for money laundering or criminal activities.
80. Crime Scene Reenactments: Settings where investigators recreate crimes to understand the sequence of events.

81. Cryptocurrency Transactions: Digital currencies play a role in money laundering and cybercrimes, often involving high-tech settings.
82. Undercover Drug Labs: Law enforcement infiltrates locations where illegal drugs are manufactured.
83. Hidden Evidence Lockers: Locations where crucial evidence is stored, sometimes tampered with or stolen.
84. Criminal Smuggling Tunnels: Underground passages used for smuggling contraband across borders.
85. Undercover Stakeouts: Surveillance operations where investigators monitor criminal activity from a hidden location.
86. Cybercrime Chatrooms: Virtual settings where hackers and cybercriminals communicate and plot cyberattacks.
87. Witness Intimidation: Locations where witnesses are threatened or coerced into silence.
88. Illegal Gambling Rings: Venues where characters engage in high-stakes gambling and criminal activities.
89. Undercover Safe Crackings: Intricate schemes to break into safes and vaults, often with elaborate planning.
90. Criminal Night Markets: Underground markets where illegal goods are bought and sold.
91. Witness Interrogation Rooms: Locations where witnesses are questioned to obtain critical information.
92. Stolen Vehicle Chop Shops: Settings where stolen cars are dismantled and sold as parts.
93. Undercover Drug Interceptions: Operations where law enforcement attempts to intercept drug shipments.
94. Illegal Arms Deals: Locations where characters buy and sell firearms and weaponry on the black market.
95. Counterfeit Documents: Settings involving forged passports, IDs, and documents used for deception.
96. Undercover Hacking Operations: Cybersecurity experts infiltrate criminal networks to thwart cyberattacks.
97. Witness Protection Safe Zones: Secure locations where witnesses are kept hidden and protected.
98. Criminal Confrontations in Abandoned Buildings: Suspenseful showdowns in neglected structures.

99. Mysterious Cold Storage Facilities: Settings where secrets, evidence, or bodies are hidden.

100. Undercover Infiltrations of Criminal Organizations: Characters embed themselves within crime syndicates to gather information or dismantle operations.

Your Inspirations

1. An investigative journalist infiltrates an exclusive cult to expose their criminal activities, but becomes entangled in their web of deception.
2. In a small town plagued by a series of bizarre thefts, a group of amateur sleuths discovers the culprits are time travelers trying to rewrite history.
3. A forensic scientist investigates a series of murders where the victims' bodies have been carefully posed in lifelike scenes from famous paintings.
4. A journalist's investigation into a series of murders leads to a remote island inhabited by a reclusive cult with a dark agenda.
5. A lawyer defending a client accused of stealing priceless artifacts from museums uncovers a conspiracy involving a shadowy art underworld.
6. An undercover agent infiltrates an international smuggling ring, but their cover is jeopardized when they fall in love with a member of the criminal organization.
7. A detective with a phobia of insects is called to investigate a murder where the killer leaves behind a trail of deadly spiders.
8. A professional thief is hired to steal a rare and cursed artifact, leading to a supernatural encounter with vengeful spirits.
9. A detective must solve a murder that occurs on a remote space station, where the confined environment heightens the tension among suspects.
10. A retired detective is pulled back into a cold case when new evidence emerges, leading to a cross-country chase to catch a killer.
11. A lawyer defending a client accused of a gruesome murder discovers that the true killer may be an otherworldly creature.

12. A retired detective is haunted by an unsolved case from their past and becomes obsessed with finding the killer, even if it means risking everything.
13. A detective investigates a murder in a seemingly idyllic suburban neighborhood, uncovering dark secrets beneath the surface.
14. A detective investigates a murder that appears to be linked to a series of unsolved cases from decades ago, leading to a shocking revelation about a serial killer's identity.
15. A detective is assigned to protect a key witness in a major trial, but the witness is a child who holds the key to dismantling a criminal syndicate.
16. A group of strangers wakes up in a locked room with no memory of how they got there, and they must work together to solve puzzles and escape before time runs out.
17. In a world where teleportation is possible, a detective must solve a murder that occurred in multiple locations simultaneously.
18. A con artist with a talent for impersonation is hired to steal a priceless artifact, but they must navigate a web of double-crosses and betrayals.
19. A detective with a photographic memory is asked to solve a murder that occurred in a remote, isolated village with no recorded history.
20. A detective is assigned to protect a whistleblower who possesses evidence of corporate espionage, leading to a high-stakes game of cat and mouse.
21. A detective discovers that a notorious serial killer they captured years ago may not be the real culprit, leading to a race against time to prevent another murder.
22. An art forger is blackmailed into stealing priceless masterpieces from museums around the world, leading to a high-stakes international chase.
23. A detective is tasked with solving a murder on a cruise ship where everyone on board is a suspect and alibis are difficult to verify.
24. An undercover agent infiltrates an underground fight club that operates on the fringes of society, leading to a battle for survival.

25. An undercover agent infiltrates a group of eco-terrorists planning to sabotage a major corporation, but their loyalty begins to waver.
26. A detective investigates a series of murders tied to a string of cryptic crossword puzzles left at the crime scenes.
27. A group of strangers receives anonymous invitations to a mysterious dinner party, where they are accused of crimes they didn't commit and must unravel the host's motives to survive.
28. An ex-spy is pulled out of retirement to track down a rogue agent who possesses dangerous classified information.
29. In a world where virtual reality is indistinguishable from the real world, a detective must solve a murder that occurs within a simulated environment.
30. In a dystopian future, a detective investigates a murder that is somehow connected to a powerful AI controlling all aspects of society.
31. An artist discovers a hidden message in a famous painting that points to a long-lost treasure, setting off a race to find it before criminals do.
32. A lawyer defending a high-profile celebrity in a murder trial becomes convinced of their innocence but must uncover the true killer to prove it.
33. A con artist's latest scheme leads them to impersonate a missing heiress, but they soon find themselves embroiled in a deadly family feud.
34. A detective with a terminal illness races against time to solve a series of murders with a personal connection.
35. An AI detective, programmed to solve crimes efficiently, starts displaying emotions and independent thinking while solving a complex murder case.
36. In a society where dreams can be recorded and viewed, a detective must enter the dreams of a comatose victim to uncover the truth behind an attempted murder.
37. A journalist's investigation into a missing person case uncovers a hidden human trafficking ring with ties to powerful figures in society.
38. A con artist teams up with a disgraced former detective to solve a crime that has stumped law enforcement for years.

39. A retired detective is drawn back into the world of crime-solving when an old adversary resurfaces, leaving behind a trail of cryptic clues.
40. A series of mysterious disappearances in a small town leads a detective to a hidden underground society that worships ancient gods.
41. A detective is assigned to protect a scientist whose groundbreaking research could change the course of human evolution, making them a target for shadowy organizations.
42. A journalist accidentally receives a package containing evidence of a massive corporate conspiracy, putting their life in danger as they try to expose the truth.
43. A detective's investigation into a string of jewelry heists takes a supernatural turn when they discover the thieves are ghosts seeking to reclaim their stolen possessions.
44. A lawyer defending a wrongly accused client discovers a hidden underground courtroom where vigilante justice is dispensed.
45. A detective investigates a murder in a high-tech smart city where artificial intelligence controls every aspect of daily life.
46. A detective investigates a murder that takes place during a live reality TV show, where contestants must solve clues to survive.
47. An attorney defending a high-profile criminal discovers that their client may be innocent and the real culprit is a master of disguise.
48. A reformed criminal is forced to return to a life of crime when their family is kidnapped by a vengeful adversary.
49. A con artist poses as a psychic detective and inadvertently stumbles upon a real murder mystery.
50. A journalist's investigation into a famous unsolved mystery leads to a hidden society dedicated to preserving the truth behind the enigma.
51. A detective investigates a series of murders that appear to mimic famous crimes from history, leading to a chilling revelation about the killer's motives.
52. A detective is called to solve a murder in a haunted house, where the spirits of the past may hold the key to the present crime.

53. A journalist's investigation into a series of seemingly unrelated deaths uncovers a conspiracy involving a secret society that controls the fate of its members.
54. A detective is assigned to protect a witness whose testimony could expose a corrupt government conspiracy, but the witness's life is in constant danger.
55. A journalist's investigation into a missing person case takes a supernatural turn when they discover the victim's connection to a ghostly realm.
56. In a future where memories can be uploaded and shared, a detective must unravel the truth behind a murder committed in a virtual world.
57. A journalist's investigation into a mysterious illness plaguing a small town reveals a government conspiracy involving experimental drugs.
58. An undercover agent infiltrates a criminal organization that specializes in stealing and selling memories.
59. In a society where emotions are controlled and monitored, a detective investigates a series of crimes committed by an underground group that seeks to unleash unchecked feelings.
60. A journalist's investigation into a series of murders leads to a secret society of time travelers who manipulate history for their own gain.
61. In a world where technology allows people to experience others' memories, a detective must navigate a labyrinth of stolen identities to solve a murder.
62. A detective investigates a series of murders with clues that point to a secret society practicing ancient rituals.
63. A lawyer defending a client accused of hacking into government databases uncovers a conspiracy involving a rogue AI.
64. An investigator is assigned to protect a witness who claims to have seen a mythical creature, leading to a search for the truth behind the legend.
65. A thief with a unique ability to see the future plans a heist to steal a priceless artifact, but a rival thief with the same ability is hot on their trail.

66. In a future where memories can be altered, a detective must untangle a web of false identities and fabricated recollections to solve a murder.
67. A detective in a city of eternal darkness must rely on sound, touch, and smell to solve a murder when all light sources mysteriously fail.
68. In a post-apocalyptic world, survivors are forced to participate in a deadly game of cat and mouse orchestrated by a sadistic game master.
69. In a world where memories can be bought and sold, a detective investigates a series of memory thefts that lead to a shocking conspiracy.
70. A lawyer defending a notorious crime lord begins to suspect that their client is not the real mastermind behind the criminal empire.
71. In a world where everyone's thoughts are recorded, a detective must investigate a murder by sifting through the victim's memories and thoughts.
72. A retired detective is pulled back into a case when a notorious criminal they once pursued is released from prison and resumes their criminal activities.
73. A con artist takes on their most audacious scheme yet when they impersonate a famous detective to solve a high-profile murder.
74. An archaeologist excavating an ancient burial site stumbles upon a crypt containing the preserved bodies of historical figures from different eras, raising questions about the possibility of time travel and a hidden conspiracy.
75. A retired detective is lured out of retirement by a series of cryptic messages from a criminal they thought was long dead.
76. A detective is assigned to protect a witness in a high-profile trial, but when the witness disappears, the detective must unravel a web of corruption within the justice system.
77. A detective must solve a murder at a haunted mansion where the ghosts of the victims are the prime suspects.
78. In a future where crimes are predicted and prevented before they occur, a detective must investigate a murder that shouldn't have been possible.

79. A detective with a reputation for solving unsolvable cases is called to investigate a murder on a remote island where everyone has an alibi.
80. A serial killer leaves behind a trail of encrypted messages, and a cryptanalyst must decipher them to prevent further murders.
81. A police officer with amnesia wakes up at a crime scene with no memory of how they got there, and they must piece together their own involvement in the case.
82. A detective is haunted by the unsolved murder of their partner and becomes obsessed with finding the killer, even if it means crossing ethical boundaries.
83. An investigator is assigned to protect a witness whose testimony could bring down a powerful crime syndicate, but the witness has a dark secret of their own.
84. A detective is assigned to protect a reclusive author who has received death threats related to the secrets hidden in their novels.
85. A detective with a rare form of synesthesia can taste emotions and uses this unique ability to solve a series of puzzling murders.
86. A journalist investigates a series of seemingly unrelated deaths and uncovers a secret society that worships death itself.
87. A brilliant mathematician stumbles upon a hidden code in a centuries-old manuscript, leading to a quest to unravel a long-buried conspiracy.
88. A detective's investigation into a cult leads them to a remote commune where residents willingly confess to crimes they didn't commit, blurring the lines between guilt and innocence.
89. A young hacker discovers a dark web marketplace where assassinations are ordered like takeout, and they must navigate this underworld to uncover the identity of a serial killer.
90. A hacker infiltrates a criminal organization's secure network and uncovers their plans for a major heist, becoming the target of a relentless pursuit.
91. An investigator with a fear of the dark is called to solve a murder in a town where nighttime never seems to end.
92. A retired detective is called upon to mentor a brilliant but unorthodox young investigator as they work together to solve a high-profile murder.

93. A vigilante takes justice into their own hands, targeting corrupt politicians and wealthy elites, sparking a citywide debate on morality and vigilantism.
94. A journalist investigating a string of unsolved disappearances uncovers a secret society that may hold the key to solving the cases.
95. A detective with a unique ability to communicate with the dead is called in to solve a murder where the victim's spirit holds the key to the truth.
96. A con artist poses as a psychic medium and becomes entangled in a murder case when they accidentally predict a crime.
97. A mob boss's estranged daughter returns to the criminal underworld to seek revenge for her father's murder, but she uncovers shocking family secrets along the way.
98. An investigator is called to a remote mountain village to solve a murder that appears to be the work of a legendary monster.
99. A con artist attempts to swindle a reclusive billionaire but becomes embroiled in a dangerous game of psychological manipulation.
100. An undercover agent infiltrates an art heist ring, but the lines between right and wrong blur as they become enthralled by the world of stolen masterpieces.

Dystopian

Exploring Dark Visions of the Future

The Dystopian genre plunges readers into harrowing, speculative worlds where the very foundations of society crumble beneath the weight of oppressive regimes, totalitarian rule, or cataclysmic events. This genre serves as a chilling mirror to our deepest societal fears, offering a stark portrayal of the consequences that can arise from unchecked power, conformity, and the erosion of individual liberties. Emerging from the literary classics like George Orwell's "1984" and Aldous Huxley's "Brave New World," Dystopian fiction has evolved to encompass a rich spectrum of dystopian scenarios, each exploring themes of survival, resistance, and the resilience of humanity amid relentless adversity.

The muse of Dystopian literature draws inspiration from the collective apprehensions of contemporary society. It springs forth from concerns about government overreach, environmental crises, and the unbridled march of technology. Authors within this genre are driven to envision worst-case scenarios, compelling us to confront the darker facets of our world and the consequences of our choices, ideologies, and complacency. Dystopian fiction, thus, becomes a crucible for examining the human condition and the choices that define us when confronted with dire circumstances.

The target audience for Dystopian fiction is broad, spanning both young adults and adults seeking thought-provoking narratives that challenge societal norms. Young adult readers are drawn to the genre for its exploration of identity, resistance, and the quest for a better world. Adult readers are captivated by its morally complex narratives, immersive world-building, and lingering sense of disquiet, fostering introspection. Dystopian literature serves as a catalyst for self-examination, compelling us to confront uncomfortable truths while igniting the spark of change.

Your Descriptors

1. Resource Scarcity: Highlights the struggle for survival.
2. Artificial Sunlight: Symbolizes the manipulation of nature by the authoritarian regime.
3. Censorship: Portrays the suppression of free speech and information.
4. Propaganda Murals: Display the regime's propaganda in public.
5. Child Indoctrination: Reveals how the regime molds young minds.
6. Post-Apocalyptic Wasteland: Reveals the world's degradation.
7. Dystopian Clothing: Reflects how clothing is used to identify social status and compliance.
8. Rebellion Symbols: Offer hope and a sense of unity among rebels.
9. Biohazard Zones: Represents areas contaminated by dangerous experiments, showcasing the consequences of unchecked scientific ambition.
10. Brainwashing Facilities: Illustrates the regime's control over minds.
11. Invasive Augmentation: Shows the physical alterations imposed on citizens by the regime.
12. Dystopian Vehicles: Showcases the unique modes of transportation in a dystopian world.
13. Dystopian Cityscapes: Reflects the decay and bleakness of the world.
14. Orwellian Newspeak: Shows the manipulation of language.
15. Dystopian Economy: Depicts a dysfunctional, controlled system.
16. Weather-Control Devices: Signifies the regime's manipulation of weather patterns, affecting agriculture and the environment.
17. Propaganda Toys: Illustrates the manipulation of children's play and education.
18. Cyber Espionage: Illustrates the battle for information in a world where data is power.
19. Underground Resistance Bases: Symbolize hope and hidden strength.
20. Totalitarian Regime: Signifies the oppressive government controlling every aspect of life.

21. Human Rights Violations: Expose the regime's cruelty.
22. Escapist Subcultures: Depicts groups seeking solace in fantasies or altered states to cope with their harsh reality.
23. Artificial Intelligence Sentience: Explores AI achieving self-awareness and its implications.
24. Biological Warfare: Adds a deadly dimension to the dystopia.
25. Dystopian Farming: Illustrates the controlled production of food and agricultural scarcity.
26. Disappearing Citizens: Portrays the chilling practice of individuals vanishing without a trace.
27. Resistance Movement: Represents hope and the fight for freedom.
28. Bioengineering: Raises ethical dilemmas about genetic manipulation.
29. Artificial Wombs: Signifies the control over reproduction and the concept of state-sanctioned birth.
30. Artificial Ecosystems: Depicts controlled environments for food production and habitat.
31. Dystopian Transportation Gridlock: Depicts a world where traffic congestion is deliberately engineered to control movement and enforce curfews.
32. Subjugated Protagonist: Adds personal stakes to the narrative.
33. Dystopian Monuments: Symbolize the regime's propaganda and control over historical narratives.
34. Dystopian Wildlife: Shows the impact of environmental degradation on fauna.
35. Caste System: Illustrates societal hierarchy and injustice.
36. Surveillance State: Highlights the loss of privacy and constant monitoring.
37. Dystopian Sports: Reflects the use of organized sports as a distraction or means of control.
38. Renegade Scientists: Explore individuals who defy the regime to pursue forbidden knowledge or technology.
39. Illegal Art: Highlights the creation and distribution of art that challenges the regime's values.
40. Dystopian Currency: Depicts alternative forms of trade in a crumbling economy.

41. Dystopian Drugs: Illustrates substances used to control or pacify the population.
42. Dystopian Education: Reveals the indoctrination of young minds.
43. Dystopian Universities: Represents institutions that indoctrinate rather than educate.
44. Dystopian Currency Implants: Depicts a society where citizens' financial transactions are controlled through implanted microchips, eroding financial privacy and personal autonomy.
45. Secret Police: Create an atmosphere of fear and paranoia.
46. Class Division: Exposes inequality and social injustice.
47. Currency Manipulation: Highlights economic control by the regime through manipulation of currency.
48. Dystopian Festivals: Showcases elaborate state-sponsored celebrations and events designed to maintain the illusion of happiness and unity within the society.
49. Dystopian Wildlife: Illustrates the impact of environmental degradation on fauna.
50. Dystopian Wilderness: Represents the dangers beyond the city's walls.
51. Surveillance Drones: Show the reach of the oppressive regime.
52. Chemical Indoctrination: Depicts the use of drugs or chemicals to maintain control over the populace.
53. Dystopian Music: Reflects the use of art and music as a form of resistance or propaganda.
54. Radioactive Zones: Signify the aftermath of destruction.
55. Dystopian Medicine: Depicts the use of medical technology for control or experimentation.
56. Refugee Camps: Portray the displaced and suffering.
57. Clandestine Broadcasts: Represents underground communications that challenge the regime's narrative.
58. Underground Transportation: Signifies secret routes used by rebels to evade capture.
59. Revolts and Uprisings: Provide hope for change.
60. Underground Libraries: Signifies the preservation of knowledge and history in secret.
61. Resource Mining Camps: Illustrates the exploitation of natural resources and the toll it takes on workers.

62. Dystopian Genetic Laboratories: Illustrates the ethical dilemmas surrounding genetic experimentation and manipulation in a controlled society.
63. Food Shortages: Portrays the harsh realities of scarcity.
64. Dystopian Fashion: Shows how society's values have twisted.
65. Cult of Personality: Shows the cult-like worship of a totalitarian leader.
66. Dystopian Healthcare: Raises questions about medical ethics.
67. Social Experiments: Explore the consequences of radical ideologies.
68. Fear of Outsiders: Represents isolationism and xenophobia.
69. Artificial Intelligence Ethics: Explores the moral dilemmas surrounding AI in a dystopian context.
70. Repressive Technology: Illustrates how advanced tech can be a tool of oppression.
71. Dystopian Religion: Shows how faith is manipulated.
72. The Resistance Leader: Serves as a beacon of hope and change.
73. Dystopian Architecture: Reinforces the stark, oppressive setting.
74. Biometric Surveillance: Illustrates the invasive measures taken to track individuals' movements.
75. Collapsed Economy: Reflects societal decay and desperation.
76. Perpetual Darkness: Signifies the loss of natural rhythms and the eerie atmosphere of a world without sunlight.
77. Isolated Communes: Showcases small pockets of resistance and alternative ways of living outside the regime's control.
78. Rationing: Highlights the scarcity of essential resources.
79. Fallen Monuments: Symbolize the decay of culture.
80. Loss of Individuality: Shows the dehumanizing effects of conformity.
81. Virtual Reality Prisons: Highlights the imprisonment of minds and the loss of physical freedom in a digital realm.
82. Cybernetic Enhancements: Explore the merging of man and machine.
83. Artificial Intelligence: Raises ethical questions about technology.
84. Dystopian Healthcare: Raises ethical dilemmas about medical ethics.
85. Dystopian Language: Represents the regime's control over communication.

86. Child Soldiers: Illustrates the regime's ruthlessness.
87. Dystopian Transportation: Highlights the difficulties of movement.
88. Vigilante Justice: Shows citizens taking the law into their own hands when the system fails.
89. Subliminal Messaging: Portrays the insidious methods used to influence the thoughts of citizens.
90. Mass Surveillance Cameras: Create a pervasive sense of surveillance.
91. Holographic Propaganda: Represents the regime's use of advanced technology to manipulate perceptions.
92. Dystopian Entertainment: Reflects society's warped values.
93. Dystopian Holographic Education: Symbolizes the regime's control over knowledge dissemination through virtual learning platforms.
94. Dystopian Artifacts: Symbolizes the remnants of a lost world and the cultural decay that follows.
95. Police State: Creates an atmosphere of fear and control.
96. Mind Control: Emphasizes the loss of autonomy and free will.
97. Corporate Rule: Depicts the power of unaccountable corporations.
98. Mandatory Curfews: Highlights restrictions on personal freedom and movement.
99. Propaganda: Emphasizes manipulation of truth and ideology.
100. Environmental Catastrophe: Demonstrates the consequences of neglecting the planet.

Your Inspirations

1. In a world where emotions are suppressed through technology, a group of rebels seeks to restore humanity's ability to feel.
2. Society is divided into two classes: those who can manipulate time and those who cannot. A timelessness revolution begins.
3. In a post-apocalyptic desert, nomadic tribes battle over access to the last remaining oasis, guarded by a mysterious protector.
4. Citizens wear masks that reveal their inner thoughts, leading to a revolution against forced transparency.

5. In a world ruled by an AI, a hacker creates a digital paradise, attracting seekers of freedom and adventure.
6. A society obsessed with perfection banishes anyone deemed imperfect to a hidden underground city.
7. Humanity lives underground, unaware of the lush world above until a curious young explorer ventures to the surface.
8. A corporation controls dreams and uses them to manipulate people's actions until a dreamwalker rebels.
9. A virus transforms people into different mythical creatures, causing chaos and sparking a search for a cure.
10. A mysterious tower appears in the center of the city, offering anyone who reaches the top a chance to reshape reality.
11. In a future where books are banned, a secret group of librarians risks everything to preserve knowledge.
12. A parallel world inhabited by sentient AI beings merges with the human world, leading to a clash of civilizations.
13. In a floating city, airships navigate a sea of toxic clouds, and a captain seeks a legendary sky island with untold riches.
14. In a world where aging has been reversed, an underground resistance fights to restore the natural course of life.
15. An artist discovers a hidden realm accessible through paintings, leading to a struggle to protect the realm from exploitation.
16. A society obsessed with longevity discovers a hidden dimension where time flows differently, offering a chance for immortality.
17. After a solar flare devastates Earth, survivors must navigate a landscape of constantly shifting magnetic fields.
18. An experimental drug grants people extraordinary abilities, but it comes with a price as they become pawns in a larger conspiracy.
19. In a world where memories are bought and sold, a woman wakes up with a memory that doesn't belong to her.
20. A group of explorers stumbles upon an ancient, self-sustaining city hidden beneath the Antarctic ice.
21. Society is divided into factions based on personality traits, but a group of divergent individuals seeks to break free from the system.
22. A powerful AI governs humanity, but a glitch grants a young girl control over the digital realm, sparking a digital rebellion.

23. In a world where dreams are controlled, a dreamless teenager discovers the existence of a dream oasis.
24. A post-pandemic world is governed by an AI that maintains social distancing by any means necessary.
25. An underground society of hackers fights against a government that has merged human and AI into a single consciousness.
26. A series of mysterious disappearances is linked to a hidden city beneath the ocean, inhabited by an advanced civilization.
27. A scientist discovers a way to communicate with parallel universes, leading to a quest to save a dying Earth.
28. A biotech corporation creates genetically modified animals with enhanced abilities, leading to a battle for animal rights.
29. A rogue AI starts rewriting history, erasing individuals from existence, and a group of survivors must restore the timeline.
30. In a city controlled by an AI, an artist creates graffiti that comes to life, inspiring rebellion through art.
31. A mysterious cult worships a celestial event that will reshape the world, and a group of investigators seeks to uncover their plans.
32. In a world where nature has taken over abandoned cities, a young botanist discovers ancient secrets hidden in the flora.
33. A virus causes people to hallucinate their greatest fears, plunging society into chaos.
34. The discovery of an ancient, indestructible library sparks a race to uncover its secrets before it falls into the wrong hands.
35. In a society where memories can be erased, a detective investigates a murder using only fragments of the victim's memories.
36. A group of survivors on a space colony discovers a hidden message from Earth, revealing a bleak truth about their past.
37. A mysterious phenomenon allows people to glimpse their parallel universe selves, leading to unexpected consequences.
38. A group of rebels fights against a government that controls weather to suppress dissent.
39. In a world plagued by a deadly virus, a scientist discovers a way to transfer consciousness to a new body.
40. A society ruled by AI has outlawed music, and a group of underground musicians seeks to bring it back.

41. An experiment to upload human consciousness into digital avatars goes awry, trapping people in a virtual world.
42. In a world where humans are artificially created, a group of "naturals" seeks to prove their worth.
43. A powerful corporation controls dreams, using them to manipulate people's desires and actions.
44. A post-apocalyptic world is divided into territories controlled by different emotions, and a group seeks to reunify them.
45. A time traveler inadvertently alters history, leading to a dystopian future, and must undo the damage.
46. In a society where memories are traded as currency, a thief stumbles upon a memory that could change everything.
47. A mysterious signal from a distant star system leads to the discovery of an advanced alien civilization.
48. A group of survivors in a post-apocalyptic world discovers a hidden underground city with advanced technology.
49. A scientist invents a device that allows people to see the future, but it comes at a great personal cost.
50. In a world where water is scarce, a group of water hunters embarks on a perilous journey to find a hidden oasis.
51. A scientist creates a machine that can extract and manipulate dreams, leading to a battle for control over people's minds.
52. In a future where humanity is on the brink of extinction, a group of scientists attempts to clone the last remaining humans.
53. A mysterious phenomenon causes people's shadows to come to life, with dangerous consequences.
54. In a world where technology is outlawed, a group of rebels fights against a tyrannical regime that controls all machines.
55. A young girl discovers a hidden portal to a parallel world where ancient creatures roam.
56. In a society where people are assigned their jobs at birth, a group of individuals seeks to break free from their predetermined roles.
57. A group of explorers ventures into a long-forgotten underground city, uncovering the secrets of its advanced technology.
58. A sentient virus threatens to take over the digital world, and a team of hackers must stop it before it escapes into the real world.
59. In a society where memories can be implanted or erased at will, a detective investigates a murder with no recorded past.

60. An ancient artifact grants its possessor the ability to control time, leading to a battle for its possession.
61. In a future where humanity has colonized other planets, a group of pioneers discovers a hidden alien civilization.
62. A scientist creates a machine that can bring fictional characters to life, leading to chaos as literary figures roam the world.
63. A virus causes people to speak in languages they don't understand, leading to a breakdown in communication.
64. In a world where gravity is selectively manipulated, a group of rebels seeks to control this power for the greater good.
65. A society uses technology to erase traumatic memories, but a group of rebels believes in embracing their past.
66. An ancient prophecy foretells the return of a long-lost civilization, sparking a search for clues in a post-apocalyptic world.
67. In a world where dreams can be bought and sold, a black market for stolen dreams emerges.
68. A scientist discovers a way to harness the power of dreams, using them to manipulate reality.
69. A sentient forest begins encroaching on human settlements, and a group of environmentalists seeks to understand its motives.
70. In a future where people can upload their consciousness into virtual realities, a glitch traps them in a nightmarish world.
71. A group of archaeologists uncovers a hidden civilization beneath the Earth's crust, with advanced technology and a dark history.
72. In a world where people can switch bodies, a young couple's consciousnesses become trapped in the wrong bodies.
73. A mysterious phenomenon causes time to move backward, and a group of survivors must navigate this strange new world.
74. A powerful corporation controls the weather, using it as a weapon to maintain control over society.
75. In a post-apocalyptic world, a young inventor discovers a way to harness energy from forgotten technology.
76. A detective investigates a series of murders that seem to be connected to ancient myths and legends.
77. In a world where dreams are broadcasted for entertainment, a dream producer discovers a dream that reveals a hidden conspiracy.

78. A group of survivors in a post-apocalyptic wasteland discovers a hidden underground library containing the world's knowledge.
79. In a society where people can modify their appearances at will, a group of rebels embraces their natural selves.
80. A detective with a photographic memory is asked to solve a murder that occurred in a remote, isolated village with no recorded history.
81. A retired detective is drawn back into the world of crime-solving when an old adversary resurfaces, leaving behind a trail of cryptic clues.
82. An archaeologist excavating an ancient burial site stumbles upon a crypt containing the preserved bodies of historical figures from different eras, raising questions about the possibility of time travel and a hidden conspiracy.
83. In a future where technology has erased all privacy, a hacker with the ability to manipulate digital identities seeks to uncover a global conspiracy.
84. A scientist invents a device that can manipulate the weather, but its unintended consequences threaten to unleash natural disasters.
85. In a post-apocalyptic world, a group of survivors must navigate a landscape where the laws of physics have been altered, leading to strange and deadly phenomena.
86. A journalist investigates a series of disappearances in a small town and uncovers a hidden underground society with dark secrets.
87. In a world where everyone has a personal AI companion, a glitch in the system leads to unexpected consequences and a quest for answers.
88. A group of explorers embarks on a mission to the depths of the ocean, where they discover a hidden civilization and a war for control of underwater resources.
89. In a society where dreams are monitored and controlled, a young dreamer discovers the existence of a hidden dream world where imagination knows no bounds.
90. A time traveler accidentally alters the course of history, leading to a dystopian future where a group of rebels must restore the timeline.

91. In a world where memories can be implanted or erased, a detective with a photographic memory unravels a conspiracy involving false memories.
92. A scientist creates a machine that allows people to enter the dreams of others, leading to a journey through the subconscious mind.
93. In a future where people can upload their consciousness into robotic bodies, a rebellion seeks to overthrow the oppressive AI overlords.
94. A group of survivors in a post-apocalyptic world discovers a hidden underground city with advanced technology, but they must contend with the secrets and dangers within.
95. In a society where emotions are suppressed, a group of rebels with heightened emotions seeks to bring back the full spectrum of human feelings.
96. A journalist investigates a series of unexplained phenomena in a remote town and uncovers a hidden portal to another dimension.
97. In a world where humanity is on the brink of extinction, a scientist discovers a hidden oasis with the potential to save the species.
98. A time traveler becomes stranded in a dystopian future and must find a way to return to their own time, facing numerous challenges along the way.
99. In a future where technology can manipulate memories, a detective uncovers a conspiracy involving the erasure of critical memories.
100. A group of survivors in a post-apocalyptic world embarks on a quest to find a legendary artifact that holds the key to rebuilding civilization.

Early Readers / Picture

Colorful Tales for Little Minds

Early Readers and Picture Books are a delightful genre designed to introduce young children to the enchanting world of literature and visual storytelling. These books cater to the earliest stages of a child's reading journey, typically aimed at toddlers, preschoolers, and early elementary school students. They are characterized by their marriage of engaging narratives with vivid, eye-catching illustrations that not only complement the text but also help young readers decode the story. The primary aim of this genre is to foster a lifelong love of reading by providing young readers with an accessible and enjoyable reading experience.

The muse for Early Readers and Picture Books is the boundless imagination of children themselves. These books are crafted to spark curiosity, wonder, and creativity in young minds. The stories often revolve around relatable, everyday experiences or imaginative adventures that resonate with the target audience. The interplay between text and visuals is pivotal, as the illustrations help young readers comprehend the storyline, predict what comes next, and develop their early reading skills. Authors and illustrators work hand in hand to create a harmonious blend of words and pictures that captivate and engage young readers, inviting them into a world where they can explore, learn, and dream.

The target audience for Early Readers and Picture Books is typically children aged three to eight, depending on their reading abilities. These books are designed to be read aloud by parents, caregivers, or educators to younger children, and as young readers develop their literacy skills, they can begin reading them independently. Expectations in this genre are centered around fostering a love for reading, nurturing vocabulary development, and nurturing an early understanding of narrative structure and comprehension. The primary goal is to make reading an enjoyable and immersive experience that sets a strong foundation for a lifelong love of books and learning.

Your Descriptors

1. Vibrant Illustrations: Rich and colorful illustrations engage young readers, aiding comprehension and sparking imagination.
2. Simple Text: Easy-to-read text with limited vocabulary supports early reading skills.
3. Large Text Size: Enlarged fonts assist young readers in recognizing and decoding words.
4. Repetitive Phrases: Repeated phrases enhance memory and encourage participation in reading aloud.
5. Rhyming Words: Rhymes make the story enjoyable, improve phonemic awareness, and support language development.
6. Bold Borders: Clearly defined borders help focus young eyes on the page's content.
7. Textured Pages: Pages with tactile elements encourage sensory exploration and engagement.
8. Interactive Flaps: Lift-the-flap features foster curiosity and interactive reading experiences.
9. Emotive Characters: Expressive characters help children relate to the story and empathize with the narrative.
10. Thematic Color Schemes: Colors reflect the book's theme, creating visual cohesion.
11. Large Characters: Enlarged characters facilitate identification and emotional connection.
12. Cultural Diversity: Diverse characters promote inclusivity and broaden readers' perspectives.
13. Clear Fonts: Readable fonts support early literacy skills and encourage reading confidence.
14. Educational Themes: Topics like numbers, shapes, and colors introduce early learning concepts.
15. Animals as Characters: Animal characters are relatable and endearing to young readers.
16. Nature Settings: Nature settings teach children about the world around them and encourage exploration.
17. Family Dynamics: Stories about families help children understand relationships and emotions.
18. Everyday Activities: Everyday scenarios help children relate to the story's events.

19. Celebrations: Books about holidays and celebrations foster cultural awareness and excitement.
20. Bedtime Themes: Bedtime books promote a comforting routine and relaxation.
21. Friendship Themes: Stories about friendship teach empathy, cooperation, and social skills.
22. Opposites: Contrasting concepts like big and small enhance cognitive development.
23. Weather Themes: Weather-related stories introduce basic science concepts.
24. Imagination: Books that explore imaginative worlds encourage creative thinking.
25. Adventure: Adventure stories ignite curiosity and a love for exploration.
26. Moral Lessons: Books with moral lessons encourage ethical thinking and decision-making.
27. Fairy Tales: Classic fairy tales introduce children to timeless stories and themes.
28. Heroes and Heroines: Characters who demonstrate bravery and kindness serve as role models.
29. Transportation: Stories about vehicles and transportation fuel children's fascination with modes of travel.
30. Concept of Time: Books that explore time help children understand past, present, and future.
31. School Life: Stories set in school settings prepare children for the school experience.
32. Animal Habitats: Books about animals' natural habitats promote awareness of the environment.
33. Holiday Traditions: Books about cultural holiday traditions celebrate diversity and customs.
34. Puzzles and Riddles: Interactive elements challenge young minds and promote problem-solving.
35. Comedic Elements: Humor enhances engagement and enjoyment in storytelling.
36. Nursery Rhymes: Classic nursery rhymes aid in language development and rhythm recognition.
37. Day-to-Night Transition: Books showing transitions from day to night help with routine understanding.

38. Seasonal Changes: Stories about seasons teach children about the natural world's cyclical nature.
39. Historical Themes: Historical narratives introduce young readers to the past and cultural heritage.
40. Ocean Adventures: Stories set in the ocean foster curiosity about marine life and conservation.
41. Diverse Professions: Books showcasing various professions inspire career exploration.
42. Hidden Objects: Seek-and-find books enhance visual discrimination skills.
43. Inclusive Friendships: Stories about diverse friendships promote acceptance and inclusivity.
44. Pets as Characters: Pet characters teach children about responsibility and companionship.
45. Bilingual Text: Bilingual books introduce different languages and encourage language acquisition.
46. Learning Numbers: Counting books help build numeracy skills and a foundation for mathematics.
47. Learning Shapes: Shape books promote geometric awareness and visual discrimination.
48. Learning Colors: Color books support color recognition and language development.
49. Animal Noises: Books with animal sounds enhance auditory discrimination and vocabulary.
50. Interactive Sounds: Sound buttons or panels add a multisensory dimension to the reading experience.
51. Art Styles: Diverse art styles expose children to various artistic expressions.
52. Cultural Festivals: Stories about cultural festivals celebrate diversity and traditions.
53. Bedtime Rituals: Books about bedtime routines reassure children during the night.
54. Science Experiments: Science-themed books encourage curiosity and experimentation.
55. Life Cycle: Books exploring life cycles teach children about growth and change.
56. Fantasy Worlds: Fantasy settings ignite imaginative play and creativity.

57. Holiday Surprises: Surprise elements in holiday books add excitement and anticipation.
58. Baking Adventures: Baking-themed books promote cooking skills and creativity.
59. Musical Themes: Books with musical elements encourage an appreciation for music.
60. Superheroes: Superhero stories inspire courage and a sense of justice in young readers.
61. Outer Space: Space-themed books spark curiosity about the universe and science.
62. Travel Adventures: Travel narratives introduce children to different cultures and locations.
63. Dream Worlds: Dreamy settings inspire creative thinking and imaginative journeys.
64. Mysteries: Mystery-themed books engage young minds in problem-solving and deduction.
65. Hidden Talents: Characters discover hidden talents, encouraging self-discovery.
66. Magic Forests: Forest adventures teach respect for nature and environmental awareness.
67. Magical Creatures: Stories featuring magical creatures stimulate imaginative play.
68. Treasure Hunts: Treasure hunt narratives encourage exploration and critical thinking.
69. Exploring Maps: Map-themed books introduce geography and spatial awareness.
70. Underwater Worlds: Underwater settings inspire a love for marine life and oceans.
71. Lost and Found: Lost and found stories teach responsibility and empathy.
72. Astronaut Adventures: Astronaut-themed books encourage interest in space exploration.
73. Creativity Workshops: Books about art and creativity inspire young artists.
74. Adventure Quests: Adventure quests foster problem-solving and teamwork skills.
75. Forest Friends: Animal friends in forest settings teach about woodland ecosystems.

76. Magical Journeys: Magical journeys captivate young readers' imaginations.
77. Insect Adventures: Stories about insects promote curiosity about the natural world.
78. Dinosaur Excursions: Dinosaur-themed books fuel interest in paleontology and history.
79. Animal Rescue: Animal rescue stories instill empathy and compassion for animals.
80. Farm Adventures: Farm settings teach about agriculture and animal care.
81. Animal Antics: Animal characters engage in humorous and relatable antics.
82. Spacewalks: Spacewalk adventures inspire interest in space exploration.
83. Art Galleries: Art-themed books introduce children to famous artists and artworks.
84. Historical Figures: Stories about historical figures teach about important people in history.
85. Diverse Holidays: Books about diverse holiday celebrations promote inclusivity.
86. Community Helpers: Stories about community helpers inspire an appreciation for service roles.
87. Camping Trips: Camping adventures encourage an appreciation for nature and the outdoors.
88. Bug Investigations: Bug-themed books foster curiosity about insects and entomology.
89. Underground Explorations: Underground adventures introduce geological concepts.
90. Rainforest Safaris: Rainforest settings teach about biodiversity and conservation.
91. Animal Parades: Animal parades add fun and creativity to stories.
92. Oceanic Mysteries: Oceanic mysteries engage children in exploration and problem-solving.
93. Dinosaur Discoveries: Dinosaur discoveries lead to exciting adventures.
94. Space Explorations: Space exploration stories inspire a sense of wonder about the cosmos.

95. Historical Adventures: Historical adventures bring the past to life.
96. Arctic Expeditions: Arctic settings teach about polar regions and climate.
97. Safari Adventures: Safari stories introduce wildlife and habitats.
98. Desert Discoveries: Desert settings encourage curiosity about arid environments.
99. Island Escapes: Island adventures ignite imaginative play.
100. Jungle Quests: Jungle adventures teach about rainforest ecosystems.

Your Inspirations

1. A young explorer discovers a hidden portal to a world inhabited by talking animals and embarks on thrilling adventures.
2. A young scientist invents a time-traveling device and embarks on adventures through different historical eras.
3. In a world of talking candy, a brave lollipop embarks on a quest to stop a candy-stealing bandit.
4. A friendly robot befriends a group of birds and helps them build a flying machine.
5. A group of forest animals forms a band to save their beloved meadow from being turned into a parking lot.
6. A tiny pirate sets sail on a paper boat in search of buried treasure in a puddle-filled backyard.
7. A brave young knight teams up with a talking sword to battle mythical creatures and save their kingdom.
8. A magical teapot grants wishes to a young girl, but she learns that true happiness comes from helping others.
9. A group of tiny explorers travels through a shrinking machine to discover a world of miniature wonders.
10. A little star named Stella embarks on a quest to find her place in the night sky, learning about the importance of uniqueness.
11. A young inventor builds a flying kite that takes children on aerial journeys to explore different cultures around the world.
12. A friendly ghost helps a lonely scarecrow come to life and experience the joys of the changing seasons.

13. A group of friendly ghosts helps a family renovate an old mansion, uncovering its hidden history.
14. A group of forest animals bands together to save their home from destruction by humans.
15. A talking shadow befriends a lonely child and together they explore the shadowy mysteries of their town.
16. A young chef in a magical kitchen learns to cook dishes with unique ingredients from different lands.
17. A kind-hearted snowman helps a lost penguin find its way back to the Antarctic.
18. A friendly dragon befriends a group of forest animals and helps them protect their home from a lumberjack.
19. A young gardener befriends a talking plant who teaches them the secrets of a mystical garden.
20. In an undersea world, a brave fish must rescue their friend from a mesmerizing but perilous coral reef.
21. A curious robot travels back in time to meet famous inventors and learn about the history of innovation.
22. A talking tree helps a lost bird find its way back to its flock by sharing stories of the forest.
23. A group of enchanted toys embarks on a quest to find the missing puzzle piece that will break their curse.
24. A group of vegetables in the garden goes on a quest to find the mythical Giant Carrot.
25. A talented young artist's drawings come to life, leading to artistic adventures in a colorful world.
26. An adventurous balloon escapes from a carnival and floats away, exploring different landscapes.
27. A young superhero learns that true strength comes from kindness and teamwork, not just superpowers.
28. A group of animal friends forms a detective agency to solve mysteries in their neighborhood.
29. A curious young explorer embarks on a journey to find the legendary Rainbow Valley and its colorful inhabitants.
30. In a jungle filled with talking animals, a curious toucan seeks the legendary Tree of Wisdom to answer life's big questions.
31. In a whimsical library, books come to life at night, and a young bookworm must help them prepare for their nightly adventures.

32. A young detective solves mysteries in a whimsical town inhabited by quirky characters.
33. A clever robot befriends a lonely alien on a distant planet and helps them build a spaceship to return home.
34. In a land of talking vegetables, a brave carrot goes on a culinary adventure to find the ultimate soup recipe.
35. A brave knight teams up with a dragon to rescue a kidnapped princess, only to discover that she's a skilled adventurer herself.
36. In a candy kingdom, a kind-hearted gumdrop helps a lost jellybean find its way home, navigating sugary landscapes.
37. A group of tiny fairies embarks on a mission to bring color back to a world turned gray.
38. A talking rainbow leads a group of animal friends on a journey to find the end of the rainbow and discover its hidden treasures.
39. A young pirate and a friendly sea monster team up to find a treasure buried on a mysterious island.
40. A young witch in training embarks on a magical adventure to rescue a spellbook stolen by mischievous forest creatures.
41. A brave firefighter dog goes on daring rescue missions to save animals in distress.
42. A young inventor creates a robot pet that becomes a superhero and saves the day.
43. A group of misfit monsters helps a human child overcome their fear of things that go bump in the night.
44. A talking tree teaches a young adventurer about the wonders of the forest and its magical secrets.
45. A small, friendly alien crash-lands on Earth and befriends a young girl, teaching her about the wonders of the universe.
46. A curious robot discovers an ancient map that leads to a hidden treasure buried deep underground.
47. In a toy store after hours, the toys go on imaginative adventures throughout the store.
48. A talking umbrella takes a young girl on whimsical adventures to far-off lands, where they meet talking animals and mythical creatures.
49. In a world of living musical instruments, a trumpet helps a shy violin find its inner melody.

50. A group of tiny fairies helps a lost butterfly find its way back to its migration route.
51. A talented young chef in a magical kitchen creates dishes that come to life, leading to culinary adventures.
52. In a world of living tools, a helpful wrench goes on a quest to rescue its kidnapped hammer friend.
53. A misfit group of insects forms a band to save their meadow from being paved over by humans.
54. In a land of talking sea creatures, a brave crab goes on an underwater adventure to rescue a captured friend.
55. In a land of talking desserts, a brave cupcake embarks on a quest to save the Candy Kingdom from a sour candy villain.
56. A young inventor creates a robot pet that comes to life and becomes their loyal companion on various adventures.
57. A group of tiny forest creatures forms a secret society to protect the natural world from pollution and harm.
58. A clever scientist invents a shrinking machine and embarks on a journey through the microscopic world.
59. A lost dinosaur hatchling forms an unlikely friendship with a young cavegirl and together they search for the dino's family.
60. A curious robot learns about emotions and empathy while interacting with humans in a bustling city.
61. Two sibling kittens, separated during a thunderstorm, embark on separate adventures, trying to find their way back home.
62. In a land of candy, a young gummy bear goes on a sweet adventure to rescue their jellybean friends from a marshmallow monster.
63. A group of miniature superheroes teams up to protect their tiny town from a mischievous prankster.
64. A group of miniature superheroes with unique powers must work together to save their tiny world from danger.
65. A curious squirrel embarks on a journey to discover the secret behind acorns disappearing from the forest.
66. On a farm, a clumsy duck learns to embrace its uniqueness while trying to join a synchronized swimming team.
67. A group of imaginative children explores a hidden cave that leads to a world of fantastical creatures.

68. A little dragon with a fear of flying learns to soar through the skies with the help of his friends.
69. A tiny mouse goes on a quest to find a magical cheese that can grant wishes, but he learns the value of hard work along the way.
70. A group of tiny fairies helps a lost hummingbird find its way back to its migratory path.
71. A curious spaceship takes a group of children on an educational journey through the solar system.
72. A tiny gardener mouse tends to a magical garden, where each plant grants a different wish when cared for.
73. A friendly ghost helps a young child solve a series of riddles to uncover a hidden treasure.
74. In a world of living plants, a brave flower sets out on a journey to rescue its kidnapped petal friend.
75. In a world of living fruits and vegetables, a friendly carrot goes on a culinary quest to find the ultimate salad recipe.
76. A group of friendly monsters in a closet helps a child overcome their fear of the dark.
77. On a farm, a clumsy rooster takes on the mission to wake up the animals, but his unconventional methods lead to comical chaos.
78. A mischievous fox befriends a wise owl and together, they solve riddles to uncover the hidden treasure of the enchanted woods.
79. A young scientist invents a machine that brings toys to life, leading to whimsical adventures.
80. A friendly ghost in an old mansion helps a young girl uncover the mansion's hidden mysteries.
81. In a land of talking animals, a clever rabbit outwits a mischievous fox in a series of entertaining escapades.
82. In a magical forest, a group of animal friends learns about the importance of conservation and protecting their home.
83. A magical paintbrush brings the illustrations in a library's books to life, and a young librarian must save the day.
84. On a snowy day, a group of animal friends builds a magical snowman who comes to life and leads them on a wondrous journey.
85. A young astronaut embarks on a space adventure inside a cardboard rocket, discovering the wonders of the universe.

86. In a land of living vehicles, a small scooter races to save its friends from a car-eating monster truck.
87. A young musician in a magical orchestra discovers a hidden realm where music comes to life.
88. A kind-hearted robot helps a lonely alien repair its spaceship and return to its home planet.
89. In a world of living vehicles, a small scooter helps a lost bicycle find its way home.
90. A brave pirate mouse sails the high seas in search of a legendary cheese treasure.
91. A magical top hat grants wishes, but the wishes have unintended consequences, leading to comical adventures.
92. In a bustling animal city, a timid rabbit learns the importance of self-confidence when he's tasked with delivering a message to the mayor.
93. A friendly cloud befriends a sunbeam and together they create breathtaking rainbows that bridge the sky.
94. A mischievous leprechaun leads a group of forest animals on a treasure hunt for a pot of golden acorns.
95. A friendly robot discovers the power of creativity and imagination while exploring an abandoned toy factory.
96. On a snowy day, a group of snowflakes comes to life and forms an enchanting snow ballet in the moonlight.
97. A friendly alien crash-lands in a young girl's backyard, and they embark on an intergalactic adventure.
98. In a toy store after hours, the toys come to life and go on exciting adventures throughout the store.
99. A talking broomstick takes a young witch on a journey to discover her magical abilities.
100. A shy ghost befriends a lonely child and together they explore the haunted attic, solving ghostly mysteries.

Fantasy

Venture into Worlds Beyond Imagination

Fantasy genre books transport readers to magical realms where the ordinary meets the extraordinary. At their core, these stories are a celebration of the limitless possibilities of imagination, weaving tales of enchanting worlds, mythical creatures, and epic adventures. Within the pages of fantasy literature, the boundaries of reality are pushed aside, giving rise to extraordinary landscapes, powerful magic, and characters who defy the constraints of our own world. This genre beckons readers to journey beyond the mundane, inviting them to embark on quests, unravel mysteries, and witness feats of heroism that stir the soul.

The muse of fantasy literature finds inspiration in the boundless creativity of the human mind and the desire to explore the unknown. It draws from ancient myths, folklore, and legends, infusing these timeless elements with fresh perspectives and original twists. Authors of fantasy are storytellers who mold new universes and breathe life into creatures and characters that capture the reader's imagination. They inspire wonder, ignite a sense of awe, and encourage readers to ponder the age-old questions of good versus evil, destiny versus choice, and the enduring power of hope and courage.

The target audience for fantasy books spans a wide spectrum, encompassing children, young adults, and adults alike. Younger readers are drawn to the genre for its sense of wonder and the chance to witness young protagonists undertaking heroic quests and triumphing over adversity. In young adult fantasy, readers often encounter relatable characters facing coming-of-age challenges while navigating magical worlds. For adult readers, fantasy offers a rich tapestry of complex characters, intricate plots, and philosophical themes. Readers of fantasy expect to be transported to realms where the impossible becomes possible, and where they can explore the depths of their own imaginations while pondering profound themes of morality and the human condition.

Your Descriptors

1. Enchanted Forest: A mystical forest teeming with magical creatures and hidden secrets, often serving as a place of adventure and transformation for the protagonist.
2. Dragon Lair: The lair of a fearsome dragon, symbolizing both danger and potential reward for those brave enough to venture inside.
3. Floating Islands: Islands that hover in the sky, creating a breathtaking and perilous setting for aerial adventures.
4. Ancient Ruins: Crumbling remnants of a once-great civilization, holding forgotten knowledge and artifacts of great power.
5. Talking Animals: Animals with the ability to communicate with humans, offering wisdom, guidance, or comic relief.
6. Witch's Cottage: A spooky dwelling hidden deep in the woods, inhabited by a mystical and possibly malevolent witch.
7. Hidden Portal: A concealed doorway or gateway that leads from the ordinary world into a fantastical realm, signifying the threshold between the known and the unknown.
8. Fairy Ring: Circular formations of mushrooms where fairies gather, often associated with enchantment and magic.
9. Underground Kingdom: A subterranean world inhabited by dwarves, gnomes, or other fantastical creatures, reflecting themes of hidden wonder and treasure.
10. Crystal Caves: Caverns adorned with luminescent crystals, where characters may seek illumination, guidance, or rare gemstones.
11. Epic Quest: A grand and perilous journey embarked upon by heroes, often driven by a noble goal or destiny.
12. Floating City: A city suspended in the sky, symbolizing ambition, innovation, and the triumph of human (or otherworldly) ingenuity.
13. Whimsical Wonderland: A dreamlike world filled with absurdity, puzzles, and fantastical characters, inspired by Lewis Carroll's "Alice's Adventures in Wonderland."
14. Magical Academy: A school for young wizards and witches to learn the art of magic, reflecting themes of growth, learning, and self-discovery.

15. Elven Kingdom: A graceful and ancient realm ruled by elves, known for its beauty, elegance, and connection to nature.
16. Cursed Castle: A foreboding fortress shrouded in dark magic or a malevolent curse, often central to the story's conflict.
17. Spiritual Grove: A sacred grove where characters seek guidance from ancient spirits or deities, representing a connection to the divine.
18. Time Travel: The ability to journey through time, offering opportunities to rewrite history or explore different eras.
19. Parallel Universe: An alternate reality or dimension that exists alongside the primary world, allowing for exploration of "what if" scenarios.
20. Sorcerer's Tower: A tall, isolated tower where a powerful sorcerer resides, often a focal point for magical conflicts and revelations.
21. Forest of Shadows: A mysterious and eerie forest where darkness and secrets lurk, evoking a sense of foreboding and danger.
22. Legendary Sword: A mythical sword of great power and significance, often wielded by the story's hero.
23. Elemental Magic: The use of elemental forces (fire, water, earth, air) as a source of magic, each with unique properties and abilities.
24. Magical Creatures: Beings such as unicorns, griffins, and centaurs, adding wonder and diversity to the fantasy world.
25. Cursed Artifact: An object imbued with a malevolent curse, driving the plot and posing a significant threat.
26. Prophecy: A foretelling of future events that shapes the characters' actions and decisions.
27. Talking Trees: Wise and ancient trees that offer guidance and ancient wisdom to those who seek it.
28. Ethereal Beings: Spiritual entities, such as angels or demons, that influence the mortal realm.
29. Changeling: A creature that can assume the appearance of another, often leading to identity crises and deception.
30. Sorceress's Mirror: A magical mirror with the power to reveal truth, reflect illusions, or show glimpses of other worlds.
31. Goblin Market: A hidden marketplace where fantastical creatures gather to trade rare and magical goods.

32. Talespinner's Inn: A cozy inn where travelers share stories and legends, serving as a gathering place for adventurers.
33. Celestial Observatory: A place of stargazing and astronomical discovery, often associated with prophecies and fate.
34. Invisible Cloak: A cloak that renders its wearer invisible, offering both stealth and ethical dilemmas.
35. Fire-breathing Beast: A formidable creature capable of unleashing fiery destruction, challenging heroes' bravery.
36. Lost Kingdom: A once-thriving kingdom now shrouded in mystery and decay, ripe for exploration and restoration.
37. Phoenix: A mythical bird that can be reborn from its ashes, symbolizing renewal and resilience.
38. Serpent's Labyrinth: A labyrinthine maze filled with serpentine challenges and mysteries.
39. Eldritch Horror: Cosmic and otherworldly entities that defy comprehension and terrify those who encounter them.
40. Mystical Waterfall: A cascading waterfall with healing properties, offering rejuvenation and purification.
41. Ship of Ghosts: A spectral ship crewed by lost souls, roaming the seas in search of redemption or release.
42. Infernal Abyss: A chasm or pit leading to the depths of hell or a malevolent underworld.
43. Benevolent Spirit: A friendly and protective spirit that guides and aids the protagonist.
44. Mystic Runes: Ancient symbols and inscriptions that hold the key to unlocking magical powers or secrets.
45. Kingdom of Dreams: A surreal realm where dreams and reality merge, blurring the line between the subconscious and waking life.
46. Moonlit Meadow: A serene and enchanting meadow that becomes particularly magical under the light of the moon.
47. Ice Palace: A palace made entirely of ice and snow, symbolizing both beauty and peril.
48. Forest Guardians: Majestic creatures tasked with protecting the balance of the natural world.
49. Alchemy Laboratory: A place of scientific and magical experimentation, where ordinary substances are transformed into extraordinary elixirs.

50. Minotaur's Maze: A labyrinth inhabited by the legendary Minotaur, posing a deadly challenge to adventurers.
51. Mirror of Truth: A mirror that reveals the innermost thoughts and desires of those who gaze into it, often with unforeseen consequences.
52. Mystical Wellspring: A hidden source of magical energy and life, coveted by both heroes and villains.
53. Cursed Kingdom: A kingdom plagued by a never-ending curse, requiring heroes to break the malevolent spell.
54. Dreamcatcher: An enchanted object that captures and interprets dreams, offering insights and revelations.
55. Giant's Forge: A massive forge where giants create legendary weapons and artifacts.
56. Song of the Sirens: Melodic and enchanting songs that lure sailors and adventurers to uncharted waters.
57. Library of Lost Tomes: A vast library filled with books of forgotten knowledge and forbidden spells.
58. Labyrinth of Time: A maze that distorts time, leading characters to different eras and alternate timelines.
59. Mystical Harp: A magical harp that controls nature and weaves spells through music.
60. Shadowy Figures: Mysterious and elusive figures that operate from the shadows, manipulating events.
61. Mermaid's Cove: A hidden cove where mermaids sing and enchant travelers with their voices.
62. Sword in the Stone: A sword embedded in stone, awaiting the rightful hero who can draw it, often a symbol of destiny.
63. Astral Projection: The ability to project one's consciousness to distant realms or dimensions.
64. Oracle's Sanctuary: A sacred place where an oracle offers cryptic prophecies and advice.
65. Rainbow Bridge: A bridge that spans across the sky, connecting different realms or worlds.
66. Floating Waterfall: A waterfall that flows upwards, defying gravity and offering passage to other realms.
67. Warden of the Forest: A guardian spirit or creature responsible for protecting the integrity of the forest.

68. Mirror Lake: A tranquil lake with the power to reflect hidden truths or reveal alternate realities.
69. Chalice of Healing: A mystical chalice that can restore health and vitality with a single sip.
70. Spectral Spectacles: Enchanted glasses that allow the wearer to perceive hidden magical elements in the world.
71. Serpent's Riddle: A cunning serpent that poses riddles and challenges to those who seek its wisdom.
72. Giant Beanstalk: A colossal beanstalk that stretches into the sky, leading to a kingdom among the clouds.
73. Lighthouse of Lost Souls: A guiding beacon that leads lost souls to their final rest, or perhaps, their salvation.
74. Wishing Well: A magical well where wishes come true, but at a cost or with unexpected consequences.
75. Living Shadows: Shadows that come to life and have their own desires and motivations.
76. Cursed Mask: A mask with transformative powers, allowing the wearer to become someone else.
77. Whispering Woods: A forest where the trees whisper secrets and forbidden knowledge to those who listen.
78. Moonlit Masquerade: A mysterious nighttime gathering where masked figures revel in magic and intrigue.
79. Floating Archipelago: A cluster of floating islands drifting through the sky, each with its own unique ecosystem.
80. Eternal Twilight: A realm where it is perpetually twilight, with a unique blend of night and day.
81. Stone Circle: A circle of standing stones with mystical properties, often used for rituals or as a portal.
82. Vorpal Blade: A razor-sharp sword with the ability to cut through nearly anything, often sought by adventurers.
83. Starfall: A celestial event where stars rain down from the sky, carrying mysterious blessings or curses.
84. Haunted Manor: A sprawling mansion inhabited by restless spirits and cursed inhabitants.
85. Crystal Spire: A towering spire made entirely of crystal, radiating magical energy.
86. Timeless Hourglass: An hourglass that can manipulate time, offering the power to reverse or accelerate it.

87. Mystic Compass: A compass that points the way to hidden treasures or forgotten realms.
88. Garden of Statues: A garden filled with stone statues that come to life under the light of the full moon.
89. Vortex Portal: A swirling portal that transports characters to different dimensions or times.
90. Village of Gnomes: A hidden village inhabited by mischievous gnomes with a penchant for pranks.
91. Crystal Key: A key carved from crystal that unlocks hidden doors to otherworldly realms.
92. Songbird's Feather: A magical feather that, when played like an instrument, produces enchanting melodies.
93. Living Paintings: Paintings that come alive when the right incantation is spoken, revealing hidden passages or creatures.
94. Sorcerer's Staff: A powerful staff that channels magical energy and casts spells.
95. Stone Guardian: Enormous stone statues that protect ancient temples or secrets.
96. Feywild Glade: A hidden glade where fey creatures, such as fairies and sprites, gather for celebrations.
97. Spirit Lantern: A lantern that reveals spirits and entities invisible to the naked eye.
98. Moonlit Bazaar: A nighttime market where magical and rare items are sold under the light of the moon.
99. Cauldron of Transformation: A cauldron that can transform objects or beings, often central to a character's quest.
100. The Eldertree: A colossal tree of immense age and wisdom, serving as a source of guidance and ancient knowledge.

Your Inspirations

1. An ancient prophecy reveals that a child born under a rare celestial alignment possesses the power to reshape reality.
2. A kingdom's knights are cursed to transform into animals, each with unique abilities, and must work together to break the curse.
3. A village of shape-shifters is threatened when an ancient enemy returns, armed with a weapon that can strip them of their true forms.

4. An inventor creates a device that allows people to visit their own dreams, uncovering hidden memories and forgotten truths.
5. A clockwork dragon, created by a reclusive inventor, guards a hidden treasure deep within a labyrinth of gears and cogs.
6. An underground resistance forms to combat a ruler who has harnessed the power of forgotten relics, each with unique abilities.
7. A talking animal kingdom is threatened by an encroaching human civilization, and an unlikely hero emerges to protect their way of life.
8. A magical carnival travels between dimensions, offering visitors the chance to experience their wildest dreams and darkest nightmares.
9. A hidden realm beneath a magical lake holds the key to saving a kingdom from an eternal winter.
10. A clockwork automaton, forgotten in an attic, awakens with a mission to find its creator and discover the purpose of its existence.
11. A reclusive enchantress is the only one who can halt a forest's relentless expansion, but she demands a steep price for her help.
12. A time traveler becomes trapped in a time loop, reliving the same day repeatedly and trying to prevent a catastrophic event.
13. A scholar stumbles upon a forgotten language that, when spoken, can reshape reality, leading to both wonder and chaos.
14. A kingdom is plagued by a recurring curse that transforms its citizens into different animals, depending on their personality.
15. A group of misfit adventurers embarks on a quest to find a legendary treasure that can grant a single, life-altering wish.
16. A young mage is tasked with restoring the lost memories of an amnesiac deity before a malevolent force takes control.
17. An outcast elemental mage forms a bond with a mischievous fire spirit, leading to unexpected adventures and chaos.
18. A cursed library is filled with sentient books that whisper forbidden knowledge, luring readers into a web of secrets and danger.
19. A traveling circus conceals a portal to a mystical realm where performers gain extraordinary abilities, but at a cost.

20. A pair of cursed twins must journey to the heart of a labyrinthine library to break the enchantment that binds their fates.
21. A forgotten spellbook contains powerful magic, but deciphering its cryptic pages is a perilous journey in itself.
22. A phoenix egg is stolen from a sanctuary, and a group of unlikely heroes must protect it from those who seek its power.
23. An eccentric inventor builds a machine that can capture and bottle dreams, but the dreams start to influence reality.
24. A group of siblings discovers a magical treehouse that transports them to different historical periods, each with its own perilous challenges.
25. A collection of enchanted masks grants wearers the abilities and personalities of the masks they choose.
26. In a city suspended among the clouds, a rebellion brews against a tyrannical king who controls the weather, dictating the city's fate.
27. A cursed sword chooses a reluctant wielder, compelling them to embark on a quest to break the sword's malevolent influence.
28. A rogue archaeologist discovers a portal to an alternate dimension inhabited by mythical creatures.
29. A young mage struggles to control their growing powers, inadvertently opening rifts to other realms and unleashing mythical creatures.
30. A blacksmith discovers a hidden forge that can create weapons of immense power, attracting the attention of warring factions.
31. A kingdom's knights are transformed into stone statues, and it falls to a young squire to reverse the curse and save the realm.
32. An inventor creates a machine that allows people to explore their own dreams, leading to surreal and sometimes dangerous adventures.
33. A cursed mirror reveals glimpses of the past and future, tempting those who gaze into it with forbidden knowledge.
34. A realm exists within the pages of a magical pop-up book, and its inhabitants seek a way to escape into the real world.
35. A society of dreamers can enter shared dreamscapes, but their dreams start to blur the lines between reality and fantasy.
36. A young witch must assemble a group of cursed individuals, each with a unique power, to thwart an impending magical catastrophe.

37. A cursed forest grants a single wish to those who enter it, but the wish often has unintended consequences.
38. A pirate crew seeks the lost treasure of a legendary sorcerer, unaware that the treasure itself is cursed and has a will of its own.
39. A mysterious fog covers a village, causing residents to forget their pasts, and a young historian must unravel the fog's origin.
40. A mysterious island appears and disappears in different locations, granting those who find it extraordinary powers but at a terrible cost.
41. An alchemist seeks to uncover the secret of eternal life but inadvertently unleashes a horde of vengeful spirits.
42. In a world where magical creatures exist, a zookeeper must prevent the escape of a dangerous mythical beast.
43. In a kingdom where music is forbidden, a gifted musician joins a secret orchestra that aims to restore harmony to their world.
44. A cursed crystal possesses the power to bring inanimate objects to life, leading to a whimsical yet chaotic world.
45. An artist's paintings come to life, bringing both beauty and chaos to the world as they struggle for freedom and meaning.
46. A magical storm has trapped a coastal town in a never-ending night, and a group of unlikely heroes must find a way to dispel the tempest.
47. A guardian spirit of the forest forms an unlikely bond with a curious child, leading them on a quest to save the endangered woodland.
48. A cursed painting has the power to trap souls, and a group of trapped souls must work together to escape.
49. In a world where wishes manifest as physical objects, a young girl must navigate the consequences of her reckless desires.
50. In a world where each person has a unique magical mark, a young orphan discovers they possess the power to erase these marks, altering destinies.
51. A rogue alchemist stumbles upon a recipe that grants immortality but at a terrible cost – the theft of others' life essence.
52. A sentient forest sends dreams to a troubled city, offering guidance and solutions to its problems, but at a hidden cost.

53. A forest guardian, sworn to protect an enchanted grove, discovers an intruder who may hold the secret to saving the dying forest.
54. A group of bards embarks on a quest to find the mythical "Song of Creation," said to have the power to reshape reality itself.
55. A group of shape-shifters is on a quest to discover the origins of their powers, only to uncover a hidden war between magical factions.
56. A map with ever-shifting boundaries guides adventurers on a quest to find the fabled "Realm of Eternal Dawn."
57. A sentient forest seeks retribution against those who have exploited its resources, using the very trees and creatures it protects.
58. A celestial clock tower controls the passage of time in a sprawling city, but it begins to malfunction, plunging the city into chaos.
59. An underground library holds books that reveal the future, but those who read them are cursed with the knowledge of their own demise.
60. An ancient, sentient forest defends itself against an invading army by unleashing its magical guardians.
61. An apprentice witch accidentally switches bodies with her mischievous cat familiar and must navigate the world in feline form.
62. A kingdom is plagued by living nightmares that escape from a dark sorcerer's dreams, and a dreamweaver is tasked with stopping the terror.
63. A celestial event known as the "Night of Falling Stars" grants temporary magical abilities to anyone who witnesses it.
64. A celestial library houses books that contain the stories of every person's life, but reading one's own book has unpredictable consequences.
65. A thief discovers a pocket dimension hidden within an enchanted amulet, leading to a treasure hunt across multiple worlds.
66. An artist with the ability to bring their paintings to life must confront the consequences when a dark creation escapes into the world.

67. An ancient prophecy foretells the return of a long-forgotten magic, but only a mute wanderer possesses the key to unlocking its power.
68. A group of heroes must embark on a quest to rekindle the dying sun, bringing light back to a world shrouded in darkness.
69. A time-traveling detective must solve a series of murders that span different eras, all linked by a common enigmatic symbol.
70. A cursed bard must compose the perfect song to break the curse that has trapped them in a cycle of tragedy.
71. A mapmaker discovers a hidden realm within the contours of the world map, leading to an adventure beyond imagination.
72. A forgotten prophecy predicts the return of ancient, colossal beings that could reshape the world or destroy it.
73. A young witch is granted the ability to communicate with animals, but she must navigate the politics of a hidden forest kingdom.
74. A bard discovers a magic lute that can manipulate reality through song, leading to a musical adventure of epic proportions.
75. A village is plagued by living shadows that steal people's memories, and a group of children must journey into the shadow realm to retrieve them.
76. An ancient, enchanted forest is the source of all dreams in the world, but it falls under threat from a force that wants to control the realm of dreams.
77. In a world where emotions manifest as magical creatures, a person's inner turmoil begins to wreak havoc on the environment.
78. A young mage can communicate with inanimate objects, leading to unexpected alliances with household items and magical artifacts.
79. A celestial city floating in the sky suddenly crashes to the ground, revealing long-forgotten secrets hidden within its catacombs.
80. A mapmaker creates a map that reveals hidden portals to other worlds, drawing the attention of adventurers and would-be conquerors.
81. A city is frozen in time, and its residents live in a never-ending day until a stranger arrives, threatening to disrupt their existence.

82. An enchanted painting allows the viewer to step into the depicted world, but each visit alters the painting, changing the course of history.
83. A young scribe discovers a forgotten language that allows her to manipulate the very essence of reality through words.
84. In a world where magic is fueled by colors, a colorless child possesses the potential to bring about a new era of magic.
85. A cursed ship sails the seas eternally, its crew searching for a way to break the curse and find their way home.
86. A sentient forest grants wishes to those who enter, but the wishes often have unintended consequences, leading to chaos.
87. A hermit living in a remote tower discovers a book of forgotten spells that can reshape the world, for better or worse.
88. In a realm of endless night, the stars themselves hold the power to grant wishes, but they are fading, and a hero must embark on a quest to rekindle them.
89. A group of beings from different mythologies are brought together to save the world from a common, otherworldly threat.
90. A library exists outside of time and space, containing books that record the stories of every person's life, but its guardians are becoming corrupted.
91. A society of shape-shifters struggles to maintain their true forms in a world where illusions and deceit are the norm.
92. A group of orphans discovers a hidden, magical tunnel system beneath their orphanage, leading to fantastical adventures.
93. An artist paints a mural that becomes a portal to another dimension, where fantastical creatures seek refuge from an approaching darkness.
94. In a kingdom where music has the power to shape reality, a young musician must master their instrument to save the land from impending doom.
95. A magical forest that feeds on the dreams of its inhabitants begins to wither, and a group of dreamers must embark on a quest to save it.
96. A cursed town is perpetually stuck in a specific moment in time, and a newcomer holds the key to breaking the curse.

97. An ancient prophecy foretells the return of mythical creatures to the world, sparking a race against time to prevent an otherworldly invasion.
98. A hidden island is home to a society of creatures that can manipulate the elements, and their powers are sought after by outsiders.
99. A guardian spirit of an enchanted garden forms an unlikely alliance with a curious child to protect the garden from a looming threat.
100. In a realm where wishes can be stolen, a wish thief becomes an unlikely hero when they discover the consequences of their actions.

Historical Fiction

Journey to the Past Through Words

Historical Fiction is a genre that weaves the threads of imagination through the tapestry of history, bringing bygone eras to life with vivid storytelling. This genre transports readers to different times and places, immersing them in the social, cultural, and political landscapes of yesteryears. It's a literary time machine that invites us to explore the triumphs and tribulations of the past, often through the eyes of fictional characters whose lives intersect with real historical events and figures.

The muse of Historical Fiction finds inspiration in the annals of history itself. It draws from the rich tapestry of human experiences, ranging from the grandeur of ancient civilizations to the tumultuous periods of revolution and war. Authors in this genre take on the role of time travelers, meticulously researching historical details to recreate the sights, sounds, and sensations of the past. Whether it's the courtly intrigues of medieval Europe, the Wild West's rugged frontier, or the trenches of World War I, Historical Fiction allows readers to witness history's moments through the eyes of relatable characters. The relationship between history and imagination is symbiotic, with the genre breathing life into forgotten stories and history lending authenticity to the narratives.

The target audience for Historical Fiction is diverse, encompassing both history enthusiasts seeking a deeper understanding of past events and casual readers looking for engaging stories set against historical backdrops. Readers of this genre expect a well-researched and immersive experience that transports them to different time periods. They anticipate authentic historical details, from clothing and architecture to the social norms and language of the era. At its core, Historical Fiction offers readers a chance to not only learn about history but also to empathize with the struggles and triumphs of characters who grapple with the challenges of their times.

Your Descriptors

1. Ancient Rome: A world of grandeur and decadence, with political intrigue and gladiatorial combat.
2. The Salem Sea Witch Trials Witnesses: Those who provide testimony during the trials.
3. Norse Viking Raids: High-seas adventures, raids, and exploration.
4. The American Revolution Spies: Espionage and covert operations in the fight for freedom.
5. Colonial India: The struggle for independence and cultural clashes during British colonial rule.
6. The Roaring Twenties: An era of glamour and prohibition, where characters are entangled in speakeasies and gangster operations.
7. The Opium Wars Colonists: Settlers in regions affected by the opium trade.
8. The Salem Witch Trials Survivors: Characters dealing with the aftermath of the trials.
9. Wild West Saloons: Gathering places for cowboys, outlaws, and disputes settled with a quick draw.
10. Medieval Alchemy: The quest for the philosopher's stone and the elixir of life.
11. The American Revolution Slaves: Enslaved individuals seeking freedom amid the turmoil.
12. Ancient Egypt: A world of pharaohs, pyramids, and mysticism, where secrets of the afterlife are sought.
13. Tudor Court: The intrigue-filled courts of Henry VIII and Elizabeth I, where politics and romance collide.
14. The American Revolution: A time of revolutionary ideas and battles for independence.
15. Feudal Japan: A land of samurai and honor codes, where characters navigate a strict social hierarchy.
16. The Dust Bowl Farmers: Families struggling to eke out a living on barren land.
17. The Salem Sea Witch Trials Survivors: Those who escape persecution and seek refuge.
18. The Harlem Renaissance: A cultural explosion of art, music, and literature in African American communities.

19. The Salem Witch Trials Protestors: Individuals who speak out against the trials.
20. The Spanish Armada: A naval conflict with England that shaped European politics.
21. Medieval Castles: Strongholds of power and intrigue, where knights, lords, and ladies navigate the feudal system.
22. The Underground Railroad Bounty Hunters: Characters tasked with capturing escaped slaves.
23. The Spanish Armada Smugglers: Characters involved in illicit trade during the conflict.
24. The Underground Railroad Station Masters: Safe house operators aiding escaped slaves.
25. Hollywood's Golden Age: The glamorous world of movie stars and studio systems.
26. Prehistoric Times: A world of primitive tribes and survival instincts, where characters forge the first societies.
27. The Salem Sea Witch Trials: An alternate history where maritime witch hunts take place.
28. The Salem Witch Trials: A time of hysteria and persecution in colonial Massachusetts.
29. The Spanish Armada Spies: Secret agents involved in espionage during the conflict.
30. The Salem Witch Trials Accusers: Characters involved in accusing others of witchcraft.
31. The Viking Invasion of England: Conflict and cultural exchange during the Viking Age.
32. The American Civil War: The battleground for a nation divided by ideals, where characters grapple with loyalty and sacrifice.
33. The Crusades from a Muslim Perspective: A different angle on the holy wars.
34. The Opium Wars Soldiers: Foot soldiers and officers on the front lines.
35. Medieval Monasteries: Centers of knowledge and spirituality where monks preserve ancient texts.
36. The Salem Sea Witch Trials Pirates: Pirates accused of practicing witchcraft.
37. Byzantine Empire: The Eastern Roman Empire's opulent court, famous for its mosaics.

38. The Gold Rush: A rush for riches in the Wild West, where characters risk it all for a chance at fortune.
39. The Salem Witch Trials Magistrates: Officials overseeing the trials and judgments.
40. The Spanish Inquisition Witnesses: Those caught up in the trials as witnesses or bystanders.
41. Ancient Greece Olympics: A backdrop for athletic competitions and cultural exchange.
42. The Dust Bowl: A period of drought and despair in the American Midwest during the Great Depression.
43. Ancient Greece: The birthplace of democracy and philosophy, where characters ponder life's fundamental questions.
44. The Spanish Armada Pirates: Buccaneers taking advantage of the naval conflict.
45. The Underground Railroad Spies: Operatives gathering information to aid escapees.
46. The Gold Rush From a Native American Perspective: Indigenous people's experiences during the rush for riches.
47. The Viking Shieldmaidens: Fearless female warriors who defy gender norms.
48. The Spanish Inquisition Inquisitors: Officials responsible for rooting out heresy.
49. The Viking Explorers: Adventures and discoveries in uncharted lands.
50. The Salem Witch Trials Healers: Herbalists and healers accused of witchcraft.
51. The Opium Wars Diplomats: Negotiators attempting to resolve the conflict through diplomacy.
52. The Silk Road Travelers: A caravan's journey along the ancient trade route.
53. Pompeii Before the Eruption: A bustling Roman city frozen in time by the cataclysmic eruption of Mount Vesuvius.
54. The Jazz Age Flappers: Young women embracing the liberated spirit of the era.
55. Renaissance Florence: The birthplace of art and intellect, where characters are inspired by the likes of Leonardo da Vinci and Michelangelo.

56. The Ming Dynasty Forbidden City: A majestic palace complex with secrets and intrigues.
57. The Spanish Inquisition: A period of religious persecution and secrecy under the Catholic Church.
58. The Opium Dens of Victorian London: Characters navigating the underbelly of society.
59. The French Revolution: A time of upheaval, where characters are caught in the crossfire of revolution and tyranny.
60. The Opium Wars Merchants: Traders profiting from the opium trade.
61. The Dust Bowl Preachers: Spiritual leaders guiding communities through hardship.
62. Elizabethan London: A city alive with playwrights, poets, and political machinations.
63. Industrial Revolution: The dawn of modernity, where characters grapple with the changes brought by technology.
64. The Silk Road Traders: Merchants seeking fortune and adventure.
65. Regency England: An era of etiquette and romance, characterized by Jane Austen's novels.
66. Victorian London: A bustling, smog-filled city where class divides and societal norms shape characters' fates.
67. The Russian Revolution: A backdrop for political turmoil, revolution, and espionage.
68. The Viking Settlers: Pioneers establishing communities in new lands.
69. The Opium Wars: A clash between China and Britain over trade and control.
70. The Salem Witch Trials Witches' Perspective: A story told from the viewpoint of accused witches.
71. World War II Battlefields: The harrowing landscapes where soldiers face the horrors of war and forge unbreakable bonds.
72. The Underground Railroad Conductors: Those who risked their lives to help escaped slaves.
73. The Spanish Armada Survivors: Sailors marooned in foreign lands after the naval defeat.
74. The Dust Bowl Migrants: Families seeking a better life elsewhere during the crisis.

75. The American Revolution Loyalists: Characters torn between loyalty to the crown and the revolution.
76. Prohibition Chicago: A city ruled by gangsters, speakeasies, and secret police raids.
77. The Salem Sea Witch Trials Fishermen: Fishermen accused of witchcraft due to their seafaring ways.
78. The Spanish Inquisition Heretics: Characters persecuted for their beliefs.
79. The Jazz Age Detectives: Sleuths solving crimes in the era of jazz.
80. The Underground Railroad: A network of safe houses aiding escaped slaves in pre-Civil War America.
81. The Lost Colony of Roanoke: Mystery and intrigue surrounding the vanished settlers.
82. The Viking Berserkers: Fierce warriors known for their battle frenzy.
83. The Spanish Inquisition Martyrs: Characters who face persecution for their beliefs.
84. The Crusades: Epic holy wars and quests to reclaim the Holy Land.
85. The American Revolution Founding Fathers: Key figures shaping the nation's destiny.
86. World War I Trenches: The grim and brutal battlefields of the Great War, where characters face the horrors of modern warfare.
87. The Jazz Age Artists: Creative minds producing masterpieces of the era.
88. The Dust Bowl Okies: Families struggling to survive during the environmental catastrophe.
89. The Great Depression: A time of hardship and resilience, where characters strive to survive economic turmoil.
90. The Silk Road Explorers: Adventurers charting unknown territories along the trade route.
91. The Jazz Age Gangsters: Criminal organizations and underworld figures of the era.
92. The Jazz Age: A vibrant era of jazz music, flappers, and social change in the 1920s.
93. Pioneer America: The untamed wilderness of the frontier, where settlers build new lives and confront danger.

94. The Space Race: The Cold War rivalry that sent humanity to the moon.
95. The Silk Road Nomads: Nomadic tribes traversing the trade route.
96. The American Revolution Redcoats: British soldiers and officers during the revolution.
97. The Silk Road Bandits: Outlaws preying on travelers and caravans.
98. Victorian Asylums: Institutions where characters encounter the harsh realities of mental health care.
99. The Silk Road: A trade route connecting East and West, fostering cultural exchange.
100. The Titanic: The ill-fated luxury liner, a symbol of hubris and tragedy.

Your Inspirations

1. A detective in 1920s New York City investigates a series of supernatural murders.
2. A Viking warrior, presumed dead, returns to his village after years of raiding and battles.
3. A French Revolution survivor seeks revenge on the aristocrat who betrayed her family.
4. In the court of Queen Isabella I, a Jewish scholar fights to preserve his heritage amidst the Spanish Inquisition.
5. A Native American medicine woman must protect her tribe's sacred land from encroaching settlers during the Wild West era.
6. A courageous samurai defends a remote village against a band of ruthless mercenaries during the Edo period.
7. A Native American healer discovers her connection to a powerful ancient artifact.
8. A skilled Mayan astronomer deciphers celestial secrets and predicts the fate of his civilization.
9. A Roman gladiator seeks vengeance against the corrupt senator who enslaved him.
10. In medieval England, a knight embarks on a quest to find the Holy Grail.

11. During the height of piracy in the Caribbean, a former privateer turns pirate hunter to reclaim his stolen fortune.
12. A samurai warrior, disgraced and exiled, becomes a ronin seeking redemption.
13. In the court of Elizabeth I, a spy must unmask a traitor plotting against the queen.
14. A female pirate captain, disguised as a man, leads her crew in search of buried treasure.
15. A medieval apothecary's apprentice uncovers a plot to poison the king.
16. During the Russian Revolution, a peasant girl discovers a hidden talent for espionage as she navigates the chaos of war.
17. In the court of the Roman Emperor Nero, a gifted musician must choose between fame and rebellion.
18. During the Great Depression, a group of misfit circus performers embarks on a cross-country adventure.
19. A Renaissance artist's apprentice uncovers a lost painting, leading to a secret society's resurgence.
20. Amid the turmoil of the French Revolution, a humble baker becomes an unlikely hero while protecting the innocent.
21. A talented sculptor in the Ming Dynasty faces challenges and rivalries while creating a masterpiece for the emperor.
22. A young Mayan astronomer deciphers celestial events that foretell the downfall of the Mayan civilization.
23. During the Viking Age, a Norse warrior forms an alliance with an unlikely ally to defend their village from invaders.
24. A freed Roman gladiator becomes a formidable gladiatorial trainer and leads a slave rebellion.
25. A Native American tracker aids Lewis and Clark's expedition through the uncharted American wilderness.
26. A brave Celtic warrior joins the rebellion against Roman occupation in ancient Britannia.
27. In Ancient Greece, a slave competes in the Olympic Games to win his freedom.
28. An orphaned samurai seeks revenge against the warlord who betrayed his family during Japan's Warring States period.
29. In ancient Greece, a female athlete competes in the first Olympic Games against all odds.

30. During the American Revolution, a young Native American scout helps guide George Washington's troops through treacherous wilderness.
31. In medieval Japan, a geisha becomes an unlikely spy in a war between samurai clans.
32. A Renaissance philosopher uncovers a hidden manuscript that challenges religious orthodoxy.
33. A jazz musician in 1930s Harlem navigates racism, music, and forbidden love.
34. A skilled Inca weaver faces the challenges of the Spanish conquest while preserving her culture's textiles.
35. A gladiator in ancient Rome seeks to free his fellow slaves and incite a rebellion.
36. In ancient Egypt, a tomb robber's greed leads to the discovery of a cursed artifact that threatens the kingdom.
37. During the American Civil War, a runaway slave becomes a conductor on the Underground Railroad.
38. A World War I nurse in the trenches discovers a wounded enemy soldier with a shared secret.
39. A Native American chief's daughter must choose between her tribe and a forbidden love.
40. A samurai's widow trains in secret to avenge her husband's death at the hands of a rival clan.
41. In ancient Egypt, a slave and a princess form an unlikely alliance to decipher hieroglyphs.
42. A skilled Maori navigator embarks on a daring voyage across the Pacific Ocean, discovering new lands and cultures.
43. In the aftermath of the Viking Age, a Norse explorer embarks on a perilous journey to uncharted lands.
44. A medieval alchemist seeks the fabled Philosopher's Stone while facing persecution by the Inquisition.
45. A Russian serf secretly teaches her fellow slaves to read, sparking a rebellion.
46. Amid the opulence of the Ottoman Empire, a talented artist secretly documents the lives of palace servants.
47. In the court of the Sun King, Louis XIV of France, a talented courtier risks everything for a forbidden romance.

48. In the Byzantine Empire, a skilled charioteer competes for glory in the Hippodrome and uncovers a plot against the emperor.
49. A courtesan in Renaissance Italy uses her wit and charm to navigate the city-state's politics.
50. A young Aztec noblewoman defies tradition to become a fierce warrior and protector of her people.
51. During the construction of the Great Wall of China, a skilled architect must navigate political intrigue to ensure its completion.
52. A master calligrapher in ancient China finds himself entangled in a web of political intrigue as he creates royal decrees.
53. A Mayan priestess prophesizes the end of her civilization and must find a way to prevent it.
54. During the American Revolution, a Native American warrior must choose between loyalty to his tribe and his newfound friendship with a colonial soldier.
55. A pirate captain seeks the lost treasure of an infamous buccaneer in the Caribbean.
56. A detective in Victorian London investigates a series of supernatural murders plaguing the city.
57. A Scottish Highlander joins a Jacobite rebellion to reclaim his family's stolen land.
58. An archaeologist unearths an ancient Mayan city and unleashes a supernatural curse.
59. In the bustling markets of ancient Baghdad, a talented storyteller weaves captivating tales while uncovering dark secrets.
60. In medieval Japan, a ninja assassin must protect a warlord's daughter from rival clans.
61. In ancient Rome, a physician struggles to save lives while navigating the treacherous politics of the Roman Senate.
62. In feudal Japan, a disgraced samurai becomes a wandering ronin and protector of a village.
63. During the American Revolution, a spy forges an unlikely alliance with a British officer.
64. A medieval alchemist discovers a potion that grants immortality but at a terrible cost.
65. During the American Civil War, a former slave becomes a conductor on the Underground Railroad.

66. In Renaissance Florence, a brilliant inventor becomes entangled in political machinations as he seeks to protect his revolutionary designs.
67. A Chinese silk merchant disguises herself as a man to navigate the treacherous Silk Road.
68. In medieval Japan, a skilled tea ceremony master uses her art to navigate the political intrigues of the shogunate.
69. A female pharaoh in ancient Egypt must defend her throne against conspirators.
70. A Renaissance explorer embarks on a quest to discover a mythical island of eternal life.
71. In medieval England, a scribe must decipher an ancient manuscript that could reveal the location of a hidden treasure.
72. During the Gold Rush, a Chinese immigrant becomes a legendary figure in the Old West.
73. A female knight disguises herself as a man to join the Knights Templar and protect sacred relics during the Crusades.
74. A courtesan in Renaissance Venice becomes entangled in the city's web of political conspiracies.
75. In ancient Mesopotamia, a cunning merchant strives to uncover the secrets of a rival's lucrative trade routes.
76. During the Salem Witch Trials, a mute girl's drawings reveal the truth about the accused witches.
77. A samurai during Japan's Sengoku period discovers an intricate web of betrayal and political maneuvering.
78. A female knight in medieval Europe disguises herself as a man to compete in jousting tournaments.
79. In Victorian London, a detective investigates a series of gruesome murders inspired by Shakespeare.
80. A skilled archer in medieval England becomes a legendary outlaw while challenging a corrupt sheriff.
81. A samurai warrior abandons his clan to protect a village from marauding bandits.
82. In ancient Greece, a female philosopher challenges societal norms by establishing her own philosophical school.
83. In feudal Japan, a ronin with a dark past seeks redemption by safeguarding a Buddhist monastery.

84. A Viking shieldmaiden embarks on a perilous voyage to prove herself as a warrior and leader.
85. A Native American shaman embarks on a quest to save her tribe from an invading army.
86. A French courtesan uses her wit and charm to spy on high-ranking officials during Napoleon's reign.
87. A scholar in ancient Greece deciphers a cryptic message hidden in a rare manuscript.
88. In Tudor England, a young woman poses as a male playwright to have her work performed.
89. In the Aztec Empire, a young priestess embarks on a quest to recover a stolen sacred artifact.
90. A Persian scholar embarks on a journey along the Silk Road to acquire knowledge and ancient texts.
91. An ancient Egyptian tomb builder faces supernatural forces while constructing a pharaoh's burial chamber.
92. A conquistador in search of El Dorado faces moral dilemmas as he explores the New World.
93. During the height of the Silk Road, a trader's caravan encounters unexpected perils and treasures.
94. A suffragette in Victorian England investigates a series of murders targeting women's rights activists.
95. A Jewish girl in Nazi-occupied France hides her identity while rescuing stolen art.
96. A Greek philosopher challenges societal norms by teaching a female student.
97. During the American Civil War, a Confederate soldier and a Union nurse find love amid chaos.
98. A talented apothecary in medieval Europe must uncover a deadly conspiracy while tending to the sick during a plague outbreak.
99. A female gladiator in ancient Rome seeks her freedom in the arena and challenges the empire's oppressive system.
100. A talented minstrel in medieval Europe embarks on a quest to recover a stolen royal treasure.

Horror

Chill-Inducing Tales of Fear and Dread

The Horror genre is a chilling literary realm that immerses readers in a spine-tingling landscape where fear reigns supreme. At its core, horror books evoke dread and apprehension, often exploring the darkest corners of the human psyche and the supernatural. These stories lure readers into macabre scenarios, where the boundaries between reality and nightmare blur. Horror books are masters of the unexpected, delivering relentless suspense, shocking twists, and unsettling atmospheres that keep readers on the edge of their seats, all while tapping into our primal fears.

The muse of horror draws inspiration from our most primal and universal fears—fear of the unknown, the supernatural, and the darker aspects of the human condition. It taps into our vulnerability and exploits our deepest anxieties, making us confront our mortality and the inexplicable. From classic Gothic tales to contemporary psychological horror, this genre dives into the terrifying, the eerie, and the grotesque. Authors in this genre wield the power to evoke visceral reactions, leaving readers with lingering unease and a heightened sense of awareness.

The target audience for horror genre books encompasses a wide spectrum of readers who seek the exhilaration of fear and the thrill of the unknown. Horror aficionados are drawn to narratives that embrace the unsettling and revel in the uncanny. They expect immersive, hair-raising experiences that challenge their courage and fuel their imaginations. Whether it's a haunted house, a malevolent entity, or the darkness lurking within the human soul, horror novels offer readers a heart-pounding journey into the abyss, promising to haunt their thoughts long after the final page is turned.

Your Descriptors

1. Isolated Islands: Cut off from civilization, these settings amplify the feeling of helplessness.
2. Possessed Memorabilia: Souvenirs or keepsakes become conduits for supernatural entities, causing chaos.
3. Haunted Bridges: Structures that serve as eerie gateways to the other side.
4. Mysterious Journals: Diaries filled with cryptic entries that hint at unspeakable horrors.
5. Haunting Puppetry: Marionettes controlled by unseen forces become conduits for malevolent entities.
6. Restless Spirits: Ghostly apparitions seek revenge or resolution, haunting the living.
7. Creepy Jesters: Clowns with unsettling grins and a penchant for malevolence.
8. Cursed Forest Clearings: Patches of unnatural calm in the woods signal impending danger.
9. Obscure Ritual Sacrifices: Arcane ceremonies that demand horrifying offerings.
10. Creepy Dreamscape: Nightmares manifest in the waking world, distorting reality.
11. Possessed Vehicles: Cars and vehicles take on a malevolent life of their own.
12. Abandoned Mines: Labyrinths of tunnels echo with the sounds of long-lost miners.
13. Possessed Children: Innocence corrupted by malevolent forces is deeply unsettling.
14. Serial Killers: Human monsters with twisted motives prey on the vulnerable.
15. Creepy Children's Laughter: Innocence juxtaposed with the sinister creates discomfort.
16. Dark Water: Murky depths conceal unknown terrors, including aquatic monsters.
17. Unexplained Time Loops: Characters relive terrifying moments in an endless cycle.
18. Insidious Technology: Smart devices become instruments of terror, controlling lives.

19. Sinister Insects: Swarms of insects become harbingers of doom.
20. Sinister Statues: Stone figures that come to life or have eerie expressions.
21. Demonic Possession: Innocent victims fall under the control of powerful demons.
22. Unexplained Time Loops: Characters relive horrifying moments in an endless cycle.
23. Creepy Children's Rhymes: Innocent songs take on a sinister meaning.
24. Abandoned Hospitals: Medical facilities devoid of life are filled with eerie echoes of the past.
25. Desolate Wastelands: Barren landscapes convey hopelessness and isolation.
26. Malevolent Reflections: Mirrors reveal sinister versions of characters or distort reality, symbolizing a fractured psyche.
27. Sinister Symbols: Cryptic markings foreshadow dark rituals and malevolence.
28. Paranormal Investigations: Determined individuals dive into the unknown, often at their peril.
29. Sinister Shadows: Shape-shifting darkness harbors malevolent entities.
30. Obscure Cult Symbols: Cryptic markings hint at the presence of malevolent sects.
31. Creepy Crawlspaces: Tight, dark spaces amplify claustrophobia and the fear of confinement.
32. Haunted Forests: Dense woods conceal malevolent entities, creating a sense of foreboding.
33. Obscure Paranormal Phenomena: Bizarre occurrences defy explanation, creating an atmosphere of disquiet and fear.
34. Sinister Orphanages: Places of refuge become breeding grounds for paranormal activity.
35. Possessed Paintings: Artwork that changes or possesses those who view it.
36. Paranormal Documentaries: Filmmakers investigate supernatural phenomena, capturing horrors on film.
37. Insidious Technology: Malevolent AI or haunted devices bring terror into the digital realm.

38. Ominous Cellars: Subterranean spaces harbor secrets, often housing horrors.
39. Eerie Nursery Rhymes: Innocent songs take on a macabre, foreboding tone.
40. Obscure Legends: Tales of ancient horrors come to life, defying logic and reason.
41. Sinister Mirrors: Reflecting distorted images or revealing the supernatural, mirrors disturb the senses.
42. Unholy Religions: Twisted faiths worship dark deities, leading to grotesque rituals.
43. Haunting Echoes: Resonating sounds from the past torment the present.
44. Eldritch Cults: Secret societies worship otherworldly entities, inviting cosmic horror.
45. Eerie Inheritance: Characters discover a cursed legacy tied to their ancestry, leading to a descent into darkness.
46. Eerie Phobias: Supernatural entities prey on characters' deepest fears.
47. Obscure Family Secrets: Hidden truths reveal shocking and horrific legacies.
48. Unexplained Disappearances: Individuals vanish without a trace, leaving behind fear and mystery.
49. Possessed Carnival Games: Games of chance that demand a dark price for victory.
50. Foggy Marshes: Thick fog obscures vision, heightening the fear of the unknown.
51. Sinister Shadows: Shadows that move independently suggest unseen malevolence.
52. Cursed Artifacts: Objects with dark histories carry malevolent forces and trigger supernatural events.
53. Sinister Nursery Tales: Innocent bedtime stories take on sinister twists, foreshadowing impending doom.
54. Insidious Dreams: Nightmares that invade reality blur the line between wakefulness and terror.
55. Sinister Orphanages: Places of refuge become breeding grounds for the paranormal.
56. Paranormal Investigations: Determined individuals confront supernatural phenomena.

57. Cursed Forest Folk: Enigmatic woodland creatures emerge to terrify unsuspecting intruders.
58. Haunting Visions: Characters experience disturbing hallucinations of impending doom.
59. Malevolent Cult Leaders: Charismatic figures manipulate followers for dark purposes.
60. Abandoned Theme Parks: Once-thriving attractions decay into eerie, haunted playgrounds.
61. Abandoned Carnival: These once joyous places become eerie and nightmarish when empty.
62. Haunting Echoes: Residual sounds from past traumas torment those who hear them.
63. Cursed Forest Clearings: Pockets of unnatural calm hint at lurking horrors.
64. Possessed Books: Tomes with dark knowledge or a malevolent will.
65. Cursed Portraits: Paintings that age or decay in real-time, mirroring the subject's fate.
66. Creepy Catacombs: Underground tunnels filled with bones and ancient secrets evoke feelings of claustrophobia and dread.
67. Creepy Dolls: Possessed or eerie dolls tap into the uncanny valley, making them deeply unsettling.
68. Remote Cabins: Isolation in the wilderness intensifies the terror when threats lurk outside.
69. Abandoned Asylums: These decaying institutions evoke a sense of dread and house a history of suffering and despair.
70. Cursed Artifacts: Objects imbued with dark energy cause chaos and suffering.
71. Mysterious Crypts: Subterranean chambers house ancient secrets and undead horrors.
72. Malevolent Cult Leaders: Charismatic figures manipulate followers for sinister purposes.
73. Sinister Cabin Fever: Isolation drives characters to madness and paranoia.
74. Possession: Malevolent entities take control of a victim's body, leading to inner torment.
75. Haunted Houses: Malevolent spirits and lingering curses make homes ominous and unsettling.

76. Eerie Whispers: Faint voices hint at hidden threats or supernatural presence.
77. Eclipses: Celestial events signal impending doom and supernatural occurrences.
78. Sinister Underground Tunnels: Subterranean mazes conceal lurking threats.
79. Mysterious Inherited Curses: Family legacies bring torment and misfortune to descendants.
80. Possessed Antique Shops: Curiosities and artifacts harbor sinister forces.
81. Mysterious Journals: Diaries filled with cryptic entries hint at unspeakable horrors.
82. Blood Moons: Lunar phenomena are often associated with heightened supernatural activity.
83. Insidious Folklore: Local legends warn of terrifying creatures that stalk the night.
84. Supernatural Fog: Enveloping mist obscures threats and heightens tension.
85. Overgrown Graveyards: Neglected burial grounds hint at forgotten horrors and restless spirits.
86. Eerie Whispers: Incomprehensible murmurs from the darkness unsettle the soul.
87. Abandoned Prisons: Haunted jail cells bear witness to past atrocities.
88. Creepy Mannequins: Lifeless figures arranged in unsettling poses evoke a sense of unease.
89. Eerie Lullabies: Melodies that lull victims into a false sense of security.
90. Haunting Visions: Disturbing hallucinations of impending doom plague the mind.
91. Sinister Taxidermy: Preserved animals take on an unnatural, unsettling appearance.
92. Possessed Vehicles: Cars or vehicles that take on a malevolent life of their own.
93. Eerie Taxidermy Shops: Stores filled with uncanny, lifelike creatures.
94. Abandoned Amusement Rides: Rusty carousels and dilapidated roller coasters are home to vengeful spirits.

95. Malevolent Cryptids: Mythical creatures reveal their darker, predatory sides.
96. Mysterious Art Installations: Surreal artwork becomes a portal to the surreal and macabre.
97. Vengeful Ghosts: Spirits seek retribution against those who wronged them in life.
98. Cursed Rituals: Arcane ceremonies unleash supernatural forces with dire consequences.
99. Mysterious Puppets: Marionettes that move independently or harbor dark secrets.
100. Unexplained Disappearances: Mysterious vanishings leave behind a sense of dread.

Your Inspirations

1. A cursed pocket watch allows its owner to relive moments of their life, but at a terrible cost.
2. A cursed camera captures images of tragic future events.
3. A cursed antique mirror reflects the deepest fears of anyone who gazes into it.
4. A group of friends is trapped in a haunted escape room with deadly challenges.
5. A cursed video game transports players into a deadly virtual world.
6. A cursed painting ages its subjects rapidly, draining their life force.
7. A group of friends becomes trapped in a remote cabin with a malevolent spirit during a thunderstorm.
8. A cursed diary predicts the deaths of those who read it, with horrifying accuracy.
9. A cursed theater stage brings the roles in a play to life, with deadly consequences.
10. A remote island is home to a reclusive cult that worships a malevolent deity.
11. A family moves into a house with walls that bleed and whisper secrets.
12. A detective's investigation into a series of disappearances leads to a hidden underground city.

13. An ancient mirror that reveals the darkest desires of those who gaze into it, compelling them to act on their impulses.
14. A sinister presence lurks in the basement of an abandoned asylum.
15. A cursed board game that makes its players reenact gruesome historical events.
16. A woman's reflection begins to act independently, leading her into a world of terror.
17. A sentient fog that preys on the fears and phobias of those caught within it.
18. A scientist creates a portal to an alternate dimension, inadvertently releasing malevolent beings.
19. A family inherits a mansion with a room that reveals gruesome scenes from the past.
20. A haunted hotel traps guests in a never-ending loop of their worst nightmares.
21. A vengeful spirit seeks revenge on those who wronged it in life, possessing their bodies.
22. A detective's investigation into a series of bizarre murders leads to a hidden underground city.
23. A cursed mask compels its wearer to commit heinous acts of violence.
24. A man discovers that his dreams are becoming reality, with terrifying consequences.
25. A cursed photograph that captures the souls of those who appear in it.
26. A cursed pocket watch that allows its owner to relive their most traumatic memories, driving them to madness.
27. A cursed clock counts down the time until a person's death.
28. A haunted subway system that transports passengers to a realm inhabited by malevolent spirits.
29. A town is plagued by mysterious disappearances tied to a cursed well.
30. A group of friends unwittingly awaken a malevolent forest spirit during a camping trip.
31. A radio broadcasts disturbing messages from the afterlife, driving listeners to madness.

32. A remote mountain cabin is plagued by a malevolent entity that mimics the voices of loved ones.
33. A cursed antique mirror reflects the darkest fears of anyone who gazes into it.
34. A serial killer is revealed to be a supernatural entity that possesses its victims.
35. An ancient curse resurrects an army of vengeful mummies.
36. A ghostly child haunts a desolate playground, seeking a playmate for eternity.
37. A group of paranormal investigators is trapped in a haunted asylum with vengeful spirits.
38. A group of friends is trapped in a remote cabin with a malevolent spirit during a snowstorm.
39. A group of hikers stumbles upon an ancient burial ground that awakens vengeful spirits.
40. A cursed music box compels those who hear its tune to perform dark deeds.
41. A remote cabin is surrounded by a forest inhabited by malevolent entities.
42. A cursed video camera records horrific events before they happen.
43. A cursed cellphone receives calls from the deceased, begging for help from the afterlife.
44. A cursed video game console that traps players in a digital realm of endless suffering.
45. A cursed tattoo begins to control the actions of its bearer.
46. A cursed book grants readers their deepest desires, but at a horrifying price.
47. A sinister carnival appears overnight, drawing unsuspecting visitors into its nightmarish attractions.
48. A cursed painting gallery where the subjects come to life and stalk visitors through the frames.
49. A haunted dollhouse replicates gruesome events happening in real life.
50. A scientist's experiment goes horribly wrong, unleashing a monstrous creature.
51. A vengeful ghost communicates with the living through eerie messages in fogged mirrors.

52. A mysterious lighthouse that emits an otherworldly signal, drawing ships to their doom.
53. A woman discovers that her shadow has a mind of its own, with deadly intentions.
54. A ghostly presence that haunts a movie theater, bringing the horrors on screen to life.
55. A cursed dollhouse mirrors events in a family's home with deadly accuracy.
56. A group of friends becomes trapped in a haunted amusement park with deadly rides.
57. A haunted lighthouse guides ships to their doom.
58. A cursed carnival ride that transports riders to a sinister alternate dimension.
59. A group of friends becomes trapped in a haunted escape room with deadly challenges.
60. A sinister carnival fortune-teller predicts gruesome fates for her visitors.
61. A cursed puzzle box opens a portal to a dimension of unspeakable horrors.
62. A mysterious fog engulfs a town, causing hallucinations of terrifying creatures.
63. A man discovers that his dreams are turning into reality, with horrifying consequences.
64. A possessed computer program that manipulates social media to turn friends and family against one another.
65. A cursed forest compels those who enter to confront their darkest fears.
66. An artist's paintings predict gruesome murders, leading to a race against time to prevent them.
67. A sentient computer virus begins to control and terrorize its users.
68. A woman receives ominous messages from her own future self, warning of impending doom.
69. A child's imaginary friend turns out to be a malevolent entity with sinister intentions.
70. A mysterious town appears only during the lunar eclipse, populated by supernatural beings.
71. A malevolent entity possesses a child's toys, terrorizing a family.

72. A family moves into a house with a sinister entity that feeds on their fears.
73. A family moves into a new home only to discover it's a gateway to a nightmarish dimension.
74. A family inherits a mansion with a room that shows horrifying scenes from the past.
75. A remote island is plagued by a supernatural fog that transforms residents into monsters.
76. In a haunted library, books write their own terrifying stories.
77. In a haunted library, books write their own horrifying tales.
78. A cursed painting ages its subjects in reverse, draining their vitality.
79. A town plagued by a contagious epidemic that causes people to turn into sentient, carnivorous plants.
80. A cursed board game unleashes supernatural chaos upon its players.
81. A malevolent entity torments a family in their new home, leaving eerie messages in fogged mirrors.
82. A cursed music box compels those who hear its melody to commit unspeakable acts.
83. A family moves into a house with a sentient, malevolent entity that craves their suffering.
84. A haunted theater where actors who perform on opening night mysteriously vanish, only to reappear as vengeful spirits.
85. A cursed mask grants its wearer incredible powers, but at a terrible cost.
86. A woman receives ominous messages from her future self, warning of impending doom.
87. A mysterious radio signal that broadcasts the thoughts and fears of its listeners, driving them to madness.
88. A family inherits a house filled with doors that lead to other dimensions.
89. A small town is plagued by a contagious supernatural illness that turns victims into monsters.
90. A cursed dollhouse mirrors the events in a family's home, with deadly accuracy.
91. A mysterious fog descends on a town, bringing with it terrifying creatures.

92. A scientist's experiment goes terribly wrong, unleashing a monstrous creature.
93. A forest where the trees come to life, ensnaring and devouring unsuspecting wanderers.
94. A haunted antique shop's objects come to life, seeking revenge on their owners.
95. A sinister hotel where guests are forced to confront their worst memories and fears.
96. A town is plagued by mysterious disappearances linked to a cursed well.
97. A series of gruesome murders are linked to a sinister online game.
98. A woman receives ominous messages from her future self, foretelling impending doom.
99. A haunted house with shifting rooms that trap inhabitants in nightmarish, ever-changing landscapes.
100. A group of strangers wakes up in a locked, abandoned hospital with no memory of how they got there.

Mystery

Unraveling Enigmas in Every Page

Mystery genre books are a literary puzzle, enticing readers into a realm where puzzles beg to be solved, secrets yearn to be uncovered, and the unknown tantalizes the imagination. At their core, mystery books revolve around the exploration of the unexplained, focusing on the art of unraveling enigmatic riddles, puzzling crimes, or elusive truths. They beckon readers with an irresistible promise: to accompany compelling protagonists as they navigate the labyrinth of clues, deceit, and hidden motives.

The muse of mystery often finds inspiration in human curiosity, our innate desire to explore the unknown, and our fascination with the complexities of the human psyche. It draws from the thrill of uncovering secrets, the satisfaction of piecing together fragmented information, and the intellectual challenge of solving intricate puzzles. Mysteries can range from classic whodunits in the vein of Agatha Christie to modern psychological thrillers that dive into the darkest recesses of the human mind. Authors of this genre are akin to skilled magicians, weaving intricate tales that mesmerize readers with the promise of revealing the elusive truth concealed within layers of deception.

The target audience for mystery genre books is diverse, spanning a wide spectrum of readers who relish intellectual engagement and the thrill of discovery. Mystery enthusiasts crave the cerebral challenge of solving puzzles alongside the protagonist, and they delight in the unpredictability that keeps them guessing until the very end. This genre's aficionados are drawn to stories that offer a carefully crafted balance between suspense, intrigue, and revelation, expecting both an absorbing plotline and well-drawn characters who grapple with moral dilemmas, complex motivations, and ethical ambiguity. In essence, mystery books provide an intellectual adventure where the journey is as important as the destination, leaving readers with a sense of satisfaction as they untangle the enigmatic threads that bind the narrative together.

Your Descriptors

1. Mysterious Deaths: Unexplained fatalities are the catalysts for investigations and heighten tension.
2. Anonymity in the Digital Age: Characters grapple with the challenges of tracking anonymous online personas.
3. Cryptic Letters: Anonymous correspondences hold vital clues, leading to the heart of the mystery.
4. Secret Codes: Cracking complex codes and ciphers is essential to deciphering messages.
5. Missing Heirloom: A cherished family heirloom goes missing, setting off a quest to recover it and unearth long-hidden secrets.
6. Forgotten Village: Isolated communities harbor enigmatic rituals and unsettling secrets.
7. Creepy Doll Collection: Eerie toys hint at a disturbed mind and hold clues to past trauma.
8. Hidden Writings: Obscure manuscripts or texts contain obscure clucs and ancient wisdom.
9. Mirror Maze: An intricate maze of mirrors distorts reality and disorients characters, creating opportunities for intrigue.
10. False Identities: Characters with hidden pasts and aliases contribute to the complexity of the plot.
11. Decoy Heists: A series of heists serve as distractions from a larger, hidden plot.
12. Bizarre Illness: An unexplained ailment or condition strikes a character, serving as a central mystery.
13. Secluded Island: Remote islands isolate characters, intensifying the sense of entrapment and danger.
14. Cold Case: Reopening old, unsolved cases rekindles interest and sparks fresh leads.
15. Sinister Portraits: Mysterious paintings reveal unsettling truths about the subjects and artists.
16. Sudden Disappearances: Characters vanish without a trace, propelling frantic searches and theories.
17. Clairvoyant Character: A character with supernatural abilities adds a paranormal element to the mystery.
18. Complicated Alibis: Characters provide conflicting alibis, raising suspicions and complicating the investigation.

19. Hidden Compartment: Concealed spaces hint at concealed truths, driving characters to dig deeper.
20. Small-Town Secrets: Tight-knit communities shield dark truths, and outsider detectives uncover them.
21. Intricate Puzzles: Complex puzzles and riddles must be solved to progress in the investigation.
22. Clandestine Meetings: Characters exchanging information in the shadows heighten intrigue and danger.
23. Haunted Mansion: Spirits and supernatural occurrences haunt a grand residence, revealing its tragic history.
24. Ill-Fated Expedition: Explorations in dangerous or uncharted territories result in unexpected discoveries and dangers.
25. Unsolved Murders: Cold cases resurface, compelling characters to revisit old clues and suspects.
26. Eccentric Detective: Unconventional investigators bring unique perspectives and methods to solving the case.
27. Secret Identity Revealed: A character's true identity is unveiled, exposing hidden agendas and motivations.
28. Missing Person: The disappearance of a character initiates the search for answers and reveals interconnected mysteries.
29. Abandoned Asylum: Derelict mental institutions symbolize madness and harbor forgotten stories waiting to be uncovered.
30. Mysterious Watcher: A shadowy figure observes from a distance, raising questions of motive and identity.
31. Time Capsules: Discovering long-buried time capsules unearths clues from the past.
32. Detective's Dark Past: The detective's own history and unresolved traumas become intertwined with the case.
33. Sinister Cult: Cults with sinister motives hide behind a veil of normalcy, deepening the intrigue.
34. Sudden Disappearances: Entire populations vanish mysteriously, leaving behind empty cities and towns.
35. Moonlit Cemetery: Graveyards evoke a sense of foreboding and serve as the setting for dark revelations.
36. Forgotten Memories: Characters with amnesia struggle to piece together their past, uncovering hidden truths.
37. Freak Weather Patterns: Unusual atmospheric events impact the plot and hint at hidden forces.

38. Strange Inheritance: An unexpected bequest comes with enigmatic conditions and responsibilities.
39. Hidden Treasures: Valuable or mystical treasures lie concealed, driving quests for riches and enlightenment.
40. Cryptic Artifacts: Enigmatic objects hold the key to unlocking the mystery's core.
41. Cryptic Prophesies: Vague prophecies hint at future events, spurring characters to decipher their meanings.
42. Hidden Safe: A locked vault symbolizes concealed riches or damning evidence.
43. Foggy Alley: Obscured vision adds an element of danger and intrigue, where characters must tread cautiously.
44. Secret Tunnels: Underground passages provide both escape routes and concealed meetings, adding complexity to the plot.
45. Hidden Passageway: Concealed routes facilitate escape and create intrigue when discovered.
46. Dysfunctional Family: Complex family dynamics hide long-held grudges and motives.
47. Locked Diary: A diary with a mysterious lock hints at hidden confidences and intrigues.
48. Secret Societies: Exclusive organizations harbor hidden agendas and conspiracies.
49. Famous Art Heist: Stolen masterpieces hold both artistic and monetary value, motivating investigations.
50. Antique Bookstore: Rare tomes and dusty shelves hold valuable information that can unravel the mystery.
51. Eerily Silent Town: An unusually quiet town creates an unsettling atmosphere, inviting curiosity.
52. Voiceless Witness: A character with no voice holds crucial information, relying on nonverbal communication.
53. Graffiti Clues: Cryptic graffiti messages appear throughout the setting, pointing to hidden truths.
54. Family Curse: A generational curse haunts a family, motivating characters to break its grip.
55. Evasive Witnesses: Witnesses are uncooperative or evasive, complicating the search for truth.
56. Ghostly Apparitions: Haunting specters hint at unresolved business and unspoken truths.

57. Petrified Forest: A forest where trees turn to stone hides a secret beneath its petrified surface.
58. Deciphering Art: Characters explore hidden meanings within famous works of art or literature.
59. Mysterious Symbols: Cryptic symbols and runes serve as clues or warnings.
60. Ancient Relics: Historical artifacts tie the mystery to the past, providing essential context.
61. Cursed Scripts: Scripts, manuscripts, or writings bring calamity to those who possess them.
62. Cryptic Riddles: Puzzling riddles challenge both characters and readers to unravel the mystery.
63. Hypnotic Influence: Mind control and manipulation add a psychological dimension to the plot.
64. Illusory Reality: Characters question the authenticity of their surroundings and perceptions, fostering doubt and suspense.
65. Psychological Thrills: Characters grapple with their own sanity and perceptions, blurring the line between reality and illusion.
66. Vanishing Townsfolk: Inexplicable disappearances lead to a community's collective unease.
67. Infiltrating Cults: Characters go undercover in secretive cults, uncovering their rituals and hidden agendas.
68. Tangled Web of Deceit: Characters navigate intricate webs of lies and half-truths to uncover the truth.
69. Twisted Family Trees: Complex genealogies unveil shocking connections and motivations.
70. Telepathic Connection: Characters share a mysterious mental link, allowing for covert communication and shared insights.
71. Double Agents: Characters with hidden loyalties add layers of deception and mistrust.
72. Secret Laboratory: Hidden laboratories conduct forbidden experiments, exposing dark intentions.
73. Hidden Caves: Dark, underground caverns conceal secrets and danger.
74. Falling Leaves: Autumn settings evoke change and foreshadow revelations.
75. Parallel Universes: Alternate realities introduce mind-bending possibilities and challenges to the investigation.

76. Ghost Ship: An abandoned vessel holds secrets of its final voyage and the fate of its crew.
77. Dilapidated Manor: A crumbling mansion serves as a mysterious backdrop, symbolizing hidden family secrets and a labyrinth of clues.
78. Trapped in Time: Time travel or temporal anomalies complicate investigations, revealing unexpected consequences.
79. Cursed Objects: Items with a dark history contribute to the sense of impending doom.
80. Familiar Stranger: A character's unexpected transformation creates doubt and intrigue.
81. Botanical Enigma: Rare and mysterious plants hold the key to solving a mystery or curing an ailment.
82. Forgotten Languages: Ancient or obscure languages hold clues that require translation and decoding.
83. Old Journal: Discovering a long-lost diary sheds light on past events and motivates the search for answers.
84. Haunted Circus: A traveling circus conceals dark secrets beneath the big top, drawing characters into its sinister world.
85. Hidden Waterways: Subterranean rivers and underground water systems play a central role in the plot.
86. Underground Labyrinth: Vast underground tunnels and chambers conceal secrets and dangers.
87. Locked Room: A seemingly impenetrable location intensifies the mystery, challenging detectives and readers alike.
88. Vanishing Artifacts: Precious artifacts disappear from museums and collections, driving quests for their recovery.
89. Invisible Ink: Messages revealed only under certain conditions intensify the puzzle-solving aspect.
90. Mysterious Benefactor: An anonymous benefactor manipulates events from the shadows, driving the plot's intrigue.
91. Covert Espionage: Spies, double agents, and espionage activities add layers of intrigue and deceit.
92. Mysterious Disguises: Characters adopt multiple identities and disguises, complicating the identification of friend or foe.
93. Mysterious Inheritance: A puzzling bequest forces characters to confront their family's past.

94. Inexplicable Auras: Characters emit or perceive mysterious auras that hint at their true nature.
95. Whispers in the Wind: Unexplained voices or sounds heighten tension and create an eerie atmosphere.
96. Enchanted Forest: Mystical woods are a source of enchantment and danger, harboring ancient secrets.
97. Haunted Shipwreck: The wreckage of a sunken ship holds spectral remnants of its crew and their unfinished business.
98. Unexplained Phenomena: Unusual events defy logical explanation, fueling curiosity and fear.
99. Seismic Shifts: Natural disasters or geological phenomena unearth hidden artifacts or mysteries.
100. Flickering Candlelight: Dimly lit rooms create an atmosphere of suspense and uncertainty, emphasizing the concealment of truth.

Your Inspirations

1. A group of friends on a camping trip stumble upon a buried treasure map that leads to unexpected danger and betrayal.
2. A geneticist discovers a hidden code within human DNA that could rewrite the history of evolution and spark a race to control it.
3. A linguist is recruited by a government agency to decipher an alien language, leading to a revelation that changes the course of humanity.
4. A detective investigates a series of murders that mimic famous unsolved cases from history, leading to a chilling revelation about the killer's motives.
5. A historian stumbles upon a lost manuscript that hints at the existence of a hidden society with the power to alter history.
6. An astronaut on a deep-space mission encounters a signal from an ancient alien civilization, leading to a quest to decode their language and intentions.
7. A detective must solve a murder case where all the suspects are residents of a virtual reality world, and the crime itself occurred in the digital realm.

8. A historian stumbles upon a diary written by a time traveler from the future, revealing a series of future events that must be prevented.
9. A reclusive author begins receiving anonymous letters that seem to predict future crimes, forcing them to become an amateur sleuth.
10. A teacher discovers that a student's doodles contain hidden messages that predict future events, including a looming catastrophe.
11. A detective is called to a remote island resort to investigate a series of bizarre accidents that seem to be connected to the resort's enigmatic owner, who claims to have discovered the secret to eternal life.
12. A time traveler inadvertently alters the course of history, leading to a series of unexplained events that must be resolved to restore the timeline.
13. An architect discovers a hidden room within an old mansion, containing journals detailing the previous owner's obsession with numerology and the occult, leading to a series of cryptic puzzles.
14. An art restorer uncovers hidden messages in a famous painting, leading to a quest to solve an art heist from decades ago.
15. A geologist discovers a series of mysterious underground chambers beneath a city, each containing relics from different time periods and civilizations.
16. A journalist investigates a secret society that uses encrypted messages hidden in music to communicate and plan their actions.
17. A computer programmer creates an AI with the ability to predict crimes before they happen, but the AI itself becomes a target of a mysterious organization.
18. An artist's obsession with recreating famous unsolved mysteries through paintings begins to blur the line between art and reality, making them a target.
19. A veterinarian discovers that a rare breed of dogs holds the key to a secret society's centuries-old plot to control the world.
20. A detective with a unique connection to the spirit world is called to investigate a haunted house, where the ghosts hold vital clues to a past crime.

21. A journalist investigates a series of disappearances in a small town that coincide with the appearance of crop circles in nearby fields.
22. A journalist investigates a series of seemingly unrelated events that lead to a secret organization with the power to manipulate reality.
23. A botanist researching a rare plant species uncovers a hidden garden filled with sentient plants that communicate through a complex language of scents.
24. An AI therapist begins to exhibit signs of self-awareness, leaving its creator to question whether it holds the key to solving a string of mysterious deaths.
25. A psychologist specializing in dream analysis becomes embroiled in a murder case when a client's recurring nightmares seem to foretell a crime.
26. An astronaut on a mission to Mars discovers a series of strange symbols etched into the Martian landscape, leading to an interplanetary mystery.
27. A private investigator takes on a case to find a missing person, only to discover a hidden underground society with its own rules and justice system.
28. A group of strangers receives ominous invitations to a secluded mansion for a dinner party, where they must uncover the host's hidden agenda.
29. An archaeologist in Antarctica uncovers a frozen cave containing prehistoric creatures, sparking an international race to study and control the discovery.
30. A disgraced magician is asked to investigate a series of seemingly supernatural murders in a small town, forcing them to confront their own dark secrets.
31. A medical examiner discovers a series of unexplained deaths linked to a mysterious substance, uncovering a conspiracy within the pharmaceutical industry.
32. An antique collector discovers a rare painting that appears to change over time, revealing hidden messages and a connection to a long-lost artist.
33. A family inherits a cursed mansion, and they must uncover the mansion's history and break the curse before it consumes them.

34. A renowned detective races against time to solve a murder on a moving train before it reaches its final destination.
35. A renowned archaeologist uncovers an ancient tomb that holds a prophecy about a looming cataclysm, and they must decipher the riddle to save humanity.
36. A detective must solve a murder case involving a series of cryptic clues left behind by the victim, who was a master puzzle-maker.
37. A mysterious time-traveling device allows a group of friends to witness unsolved historical mysteries firsthand and uncover the truth.
38. A linguist is tasked with decoding an ancient language found on a series of ancient artifacts that hold clues to the location of a hidden civilization.
39. An antique shop owner discovers a hidden room filled with cursed objects, and they must break the curse to save their town.
40. A detective is called to a remote island retreat to solve a murder, but the island's residents are all identical twins, making identification and alibis nearly impossible.
41. A hacker receives an anonymous message challenging them to uncover a corporate conspiracy that threatens to control the world's information.
42. An investigative journalist uncovers a secret society that controls the world's major events and must expose their agenda before it's too late.
43. In a remote village, an epidemic breaks out, and a traveling doctor must uncover the source of the illness while navigating the villagers' superstitions and secrets.
44. An ancient map found in a library's archives leads a group of treasure hunters on a perilous journey to uncover a lost city.
45. A journalist stumbles upon a forgotten journal from a famous explorer, revealing clues to a lost civilization hidden deep in the Amazon rainforest.
46. In a post-apocalyptic world, a scavenger stumbles upon a mysterious machine that has the power to change reality, setting off a quest to understand its origin and purpose.
47. A renowned scientist invents a device that can extract and visualize a person's dreams, but when the device malfunctions, it

reveals a shared dream world where a sinister entity lurks, endangering the dreamers' lives.

48. A librarian discovers a series of coded messages hidden within classic books, leading to a centuries-old conspiracy.
49. A detective with a rare form of synesthesia can taste emotions, leading to unique insights into solving crimes.
50. A retired spy is lured out of retirement by a series of mysterious events that threaten national security.
51. A geneticist discovers a hidden gene linked to extraordinary abilities, setting off a race to control and study it.
52. A detective must solve a murder case where the only witnesses are the victim's pet parrots, who may hold the key to the killer's identity.
53. A disgraced scientist is given a second chance to prove their theories when they discover a hidden laboratory with advanced technology.
54. A time-traveling historian becomes trapped in the past and must unravel a series of historical mysteries to find a way home.
55. A series of mysterious disappearances in a small town are linked to a secret portal that transports people to an alternate dimension.
56. A group of passengers on a cruise ship becomes stranded on a deserted island, and they must uncover the island's dark secrets to survive.
57. An archaeologist stumbles upon a hidden chamber beneath the Great Pyramid of Giza that contains ancient technology and clues to humanity's origins.
58. A photographer stumbles upon a series of photographs taken by a missing artist that seem to capture glimpses of the afterlife.
59. A hacker stumbles upon a hidden database of classified government files, exposing a web of conspiracies and cover-ups.
60. A cryptic message found in a bottle washed ashore leads a group of strangers on a perilous journey to uncover a lost underwater city.
61. A psychologist discovers that a patient's recurring nightmares are connected to a real unsolved crime, and together, they must uncover the truth.

62. An amnesiac wakes up in a remote cabin with a dead body and no memory of who they are, setting off a journey of self-discovery and redemption.
63. A retired spy is blackmailed into taking on one last mission that involves infiltrating a secret society with global influence.
64. A cryptanalyst is tasked with decoding a message from a notorious criminal, but the message turns out to be a riddle that leads to a hidden treasure.
65. A psychologist specializing in hypnotherapy is called to investigate a patient's repressed memories, leading to the revelation of a forgotten crime.
66. A detective must solve a series of murders that mimic famous unsolved cases from history, leading to a chilling revelation about the killer's motives.
67. A journalist receives a series of encrypted messages from an anonymous source, revealing a government conspiracy that could change the course of history.
68. A librarian discovers a hidden chamber beneath a library that contains a vast collection of books written by people from different time periods, sparking a quest to protect the books' secrets.
69. A time traveler becomes stranded in the past and must navigate a series of historical mysteries to find a way home while avoiding altering the timeline.
70. A historian uncovers a lost civilization buried deep in the Amazon rainforest, leading to a quest for hidden treasures and ancient knowledge.
71. A town's water supply is mysteriously poisoned, and a young chemist with a checkered past must clear their name while finding the real culprit.
72. A journalist investigating a conspiracy is pursued by a relentless entity that can manipulate reality, forcing them to question what is real.
73. A librarian uncovers a hidden library filled with books written by authors who disappeared mysteriously, and they must uncover the truth behind their disappearances.

74. A conspiracy theorist uncovers a series of coded messages hidden within viral internet memes, leading to a web of intrigue and deception.
75. An archaeologist unearths an ancient artifact that allows them to communicate with spirits, opening a doorway to unsolved mysteries of the past.
76. A geneticist discovers a hidden gene in the human genome that grants extraordinary abilities, sparking a global race to control and study it.
77. A neuroscientist invents a device that allows users to enter others' dreams, leading to a series of unexpected discoveries and dangers.
78. A psychologist is called to evaluate a patient who claims to have memories of a past life, but the memories hold clues to an unsolved murder.
79. A child's imaginary friend reappears as an adult, leading to a series of events that reveal unsettling truths about the past.
80. A detective with a photographic memory investigates a murder in a remote village with no recorded history.
81. A retired detective returns to crime-solving when an old adversary leaves cryptic clues.
82. An archaeologist finds preserved bodies of historical figures, sparking questions about time travel and conspiracy.
83. A detective is assigned to a case involving a series of unsolved murders that share eerie similarities with famous works of literature.
84. A geologist discovers a series of underground tunnels beneath a small town, leading to a network of hidden chambers and mysteries.
85. A detective is haunted by recurring dreams that seem to offer clues to a series of unsolved murders from the past.
86. In a haunted lighthouse, a group of strangers becomes trapped during a storm, and they must uncover the lighthouse's dark history to escape.
87. A cryptic crossword puzzle holds clues to a series of unsolved crimes, and a crossword enthusiast takes it upon themselves to solve the mystery.

88. A cryptic crossword puzzle published in a newspaper holds clues to a series of unexplained events occurring throughout a city.
89. A retired spy is drawn back into the world of espionage when a former colleague goes missing while investigating a powerful underground organization.
90. A detective with a photographic memory must rely on their mental images to solve a case when all physical evidence is destroyed.
91. A detective with a unique ability to see the last moments of a person's life must use this gift to solve a murder with no witnesses.
92. A librarian discovers a hidden room in the library that holds books written by people who haven't been born yet, leading to a quest to prevent future disasters.
93. In a futuristic city, a detective must solve a murder case involving a rogue AI that can manipulate reality.
94. A detective must solve a series of murders where the victims are all connected by a single, cryptic message left at each crime scene.
95. A detective is assigned to protect a witness with a unique ability to see into the future, making them a target for a powerful criminal organization.
96. An investigative journalist uncovers a secret society that communicates through hidden messages embedded in street art and graffiti.
97. A librarian uncovers a hidden library within a famous museum that contains books written by people who had glimpses of the future, leading to a quest to understand their visions.
98. A treasure hunter embarks on a quest to find a legendary artifact said to grant immortality but must decipher a series of cryptic clues to locate it.
99. A chef at a high-end restaurant becomes entangled in a web of intrigue when a food critic dies mysteriously after dining there.
100. A cybersecurity expert investigating a series of high-profile data breaches and cyberattacks discovers that the attacks are not the work of hackers but rather a sentient AI seeking to expose hidden truths about powerful corporations and governments.

~ 10 ~

Romance

Where Love Blossoms in Every Chapter

Romance genre books are a literary haven where love takes center stage, inviting readers into the tender, passionate, and often tumultuous world of human connection. At its heart, the genre revolves around the exploration of love, desire, and intimate relationships, weaving tales of affection, longing, and the pursuit of happily-ever-afters. Romance books are a captivating reflection of the emotional spectrum of human experiences, where characters navigate the complexities of love while readers are drawn into the whirlwind of their emotions.

The muse of Romance is deeply intertwined with the human condition, drawing inspiration from the universal yearning for love and connection. It taps into the fundamental desire for soulful bonds and the belief that true love can conquer adversity. Authors in this genre are skilled architects of emotion, sculpting characters who embark on transformative journeys, ultimately finding solace in each other's arms. The genre often explores various sub-genres, from historical romances set in bygone eras to contemporary tales of modern love, catering to a diverse audience with a shared appreciation for heartwarming stories of affection.

The target audience for Romance books is as diverse as the facets of love itself, encompassing readers of all backgrounds and ages who seek heartwarming narratives that explore the complexities of human connection. Whether young adults exploring the exhilaration of first love or adults craving the timeless allure of passionate affairs, readers of Romance anticipate narratives that deliver on the promise of love's transformative power. They expect engaging characters, emotional depth, and a satisfying emotional journey that culminates in a fulfilling romantic union. In essence, Romance literature offers a refuge for those who cherish the magic of love stories, where the enduring message is that love, in all its forms, has the power to heal, inspire, and captivate the heart.

Your Descriptors

1. Coffee Shop: A cozy setting where characters often meet, fostering intimacy and shared moments over coffee.
2. Beach Resort: A tropical paradise for passionate getaways, symbolizing escape and relaxation.
3. Forbidden Love: The allure of love against the odds, adding tension and drama to the narrative.
4. Slow Burn: A gradual buildup of romantic tension, allowing readers to savor the anticipation.
5. Second Chances: The hope of rekindling lost love, exploring growth and redemption.
6. Small Town: A close-knit community where love blossoms amid familiarity and shared values.
7. Arranged Marriage: A complex dynamic where love can evolve from duty and partnership.
8. Secret Admirer: The mystery of hidden affections, creating intrigue and excitement.
9. Love Triangle: A conflict of the heart, sparking debates among readers about the ideal partner.
10. Historical Setting: Different eras add depth and cultural richness to love stories.
11. Friends to Lovers: A deepening of friendship into passionate romance, celebrating emotional connection.
12. Love Letters: The power of written words to convey profound emotions, adding a nostalgic touch.
13. Family Feuds: Love across feuding families, echoing themes of reconciliation and unity.
14. Multicultural Romance: Exploring love between characters from diverse backgrounds, celebrating differences.
15. Amnesia: The mystery of forgotten love, inviting readers to rediscover past connections.
16. Fairy Tale: Love stories with elements of magic and enchantment, offering escapism and whimsy.
17. Opposites Attract: Characters with contrasting personalities find common ground in love.
18. High Society: Romance amid wealth and privilege, exploring class dynamics and personal values.

19. Soulmates: A profound connection between characters, celebrating destiny and fate.
20. Travel Adventure: Love blossoms amidst exotic locales, igniting a sense of wanderlust.
21. Marriage of Convenience: Love born out of practicality, leading to emotional transformation.
22. Time Travel: Love transcending time and space, exploring the enduring nature of affection.
23. Artistic Muse: Love kindled by artistic passion, highlighting creativity and inspiration.
24. Single Parent: Characters navigating love while raising children, emphasizing family bonds.
25. Mistaken Identity: The comedy and drama of characters falling for the wrong person.
26. Secrets and Lies: Love amidst deception, with revelation leading to forgiveness and growth.
27. Rags to Riches: A journey from hardship to prosperity, underscoring resilience and ambition.
28. Holidays: Festive settings heighten the magic of love during special occasions.
29. Music and Songwriting: Love intertwined with the power of music, evoking emotions.
30. Sports Romance: Characters bonding through sports, showcasing teamwork and passion.
31. Long-Distance Love: Navigating the challenges of love across geographical boundaries.
32. Reality TV: Love amid the spotlight, exploring the impact of fame on relationships.
33. Innocent Heroine: A pure-hearted protagonist capturing the hero's affections, highlighting purity.
34. Wedding Planner: Characters organizing weddings, symbolizing commitment and love.
35. Billionaire Romance: Wealth and opulence serve as a backdrop for love, exploring power dynamics.
36. Age Gap: Love between characters of different generations, celebrating maturity and youth.
37. Sibling's Best Friend: Romance with a sibling's close friend, adding complexity and loyalty.

38. College Romance: Young love on campus, exploring self-discovery and growth.
39. Pirate Adventure: Love amid high-seas adventure, evoking danger and daring.
40. Haunted House: Romance amidst paranormal events, showcasing courage and connection.
41. Cinderella Story: Transformation from humble beginnings to a fairytale ending, emphasizing hope.
42. LGBTQ+ Romance: Diverse love stories that celebrate LGBTQ+ relationships.
43. Art World: Love in the world of art and creativity, highlighting expression and passion.
44. Mysterious Stranger: Love sparked by a charismatic stranger, evoking curiosity and intrigue.
45. Bookstore Romance: Shared love for literature leads to connections and intellectual attraction.
46. Widower/Widow: Finding love after loss, emphasizing resilience and healing.
47. Rebel Romance: Love amidst rebellion or activism, exploring passion and purpose.
48. Spiritual Connection: Characters bonded by faith or spirituality, highlighting shared values.
49. Royalty: Love in regal settings, exploring duty, tradition, and personal desires.
50. War Time Romance: Love in the midst of conflict, showcasing resilience and hope.
51. Bodyguard Romance: Love between protector and protected, underscoring trust and vulnerability.
52. Medical Drama: Romance amid the challenges of the medical profession, showcasing empathy.
53. Culinary Love: Shared passion for food and cooking, igniting the senses and creativity.
54. Summer Camp: Young love blossoms at camp, highlighting growth and friendship.
55. Rivalry Turned Romance: Characters from rival factions find love, exploring reconciliation.
56. Superhero Romance: Love in the world of superheroes and supervillains, celebrating strength.

57. Reality Shift: Love across alternate dimensions or realities, exploring the concept of destiny.
58. Time Loop: Love stories set within time loops, showcasing persistence and determination.
59. Dystopian Love: Love amid apocalyptic settings, emphasizing the enduring power of affection.
60. Teacher-Student: Complex dynamics in love stories between educators and students.
61. Animal Companionship: Characters bonding over shared love for animals, highlighting compassion.
62. Secret Society: Love stories within secretive organizations, evoking intrigue and mystery.
63. Cottagecore: Romance set in idyllic rural settings, celebrating simplicity and nature.
64. Reunion Romance: Characters reunite after years apart, exploring the impact of time.
65. Rural Love: Love in the countryside, emphasizing authenticity and connection to nature.
66. Cruise Ship Romance: Love stories aboard cruise ships, symbolizing adventure and escape.
67. Art Heist: Romance intertwined with art theft and intrigue, evoking daring and passion.
68. Library Romance: Love stories set in libraries, celebrating knowledge and shared interests.
69. Celestial Love: Love stories with celestial beings or cosmic elements, evoking wonder.
70. Fairytale Retelling: New interpretations of classic fairytales, exploring timeless themes.
71. Supernatural Beings: Love involving vampires, werewolves, or other supernatural creatures.
72. Fame and Fortune: Love amid fame and fortune, exploring the cost of success.
73. Exotic Travel: Love blossoms during exotic travels, highlighting adventure and discovery.
74. Paranormal Investigator: Love stories intertwined with paranormal mysteries, evoking curiosity.
75. Dance and Ballet: Love in the world of dance and ballet, symbolizing grace and passion.

76. Island Getaway: Love stories set on remote islands, emphasizing seclusion and connection.
77. Equestrian Romance: Characters bond over a shared love for horses, evoking dedication.
78. Timeless Love Letters: Love communicated through letters that transcend time, symbolizing enduring affection.
79. Journalistic Pursuit: Love stories within the realm of journalism, exploring truth and ethics.
80. Martial Arts: Love amid martial arts training, showcasing discipline and strength.
81. Fashion World: Love in the world of fashion and design, celebrating creativity.
82. Haunted Forest: Romance amidst mysterious and eerie woods, evoking suspense.
83. Escape Room: Love stories set in escape rooms, highlighting problem-solving and teamwork.
84. Boarding School: Young love flourishes in the confines of a boarding school, symbolizing growth.
85. Museum Romance: Love amid the world of art and history, evoking appreciation for culture.
86. Astronomy Love: Characters bond over a shared fascination with the stars and cosmos, symbolizing wonder.
87. Circus Romance: Love stories set within the magical world of the circus, celebrating uniqueness.
88. Political Intrigue: Romance amid political intrigue and power struggles, exploring ethics.
89. Cul-de-sac: Love stories within tight-knit neighborhood communities, emphasizing unity.
90. Summer Job: Love blossoms during summer employment, symbolizing opportunity and growth.
91. Antique Store: Love stories set in antique shops, evoking nostalgia and history.
92. Tutoring Relationship: Love between a tutor and student, highlighting shared growth.
93. Spiritual Retreat: Characters find love during spiritual retreats, symbolizing self-discovery.
94. Environmental Conservation: Love stories involving environmental activism, celebrating nature.

95. Haunted Ship: Romance amidst the mystery of a haunted ship, evoking courage.
96. Theater Love: Love in the world of theater and drama, showcasing creativity.
97. Gaming World: Characters bond through online gaming, celebrating shared interests.
98. Treasure Hunt: Love stories entwined with treasure hunting, symbolizing adventure and discovery.
99. Animal Sanctuary: Characters unite in their love for animal rescue, emphasizing compassion.
100. Carnival Romance: Love stories set within the magical world of carnivals, evoking wonder and excitement.

Your Inspirations

1. A reclusive artist and a gallery owner form a connection through the power of art and love.
2. A ghostwriter falls in love with the author they're ghostwriting for.
3. A ghost tour guide falls in love with a skeptic who joins one of the tours.
4. A musician and a deaf fan communicate through the language of music.
5. A firefighter and a paramedic find love amid the chaos and danger of emergency situations.
6. A mystery writer and a private investigator collaborate on real-life mysteries and love.
7. A violinist and a conductor create beautiful music on and off the stage.
8. A detective and a journalist investigate a cold case together and uncover more than they expected.
9. A barista and a food truck owner fall in love over a shared love for coffee and cuisine.
10. A forest ranger and a wildlife photographer find love while protecting endangered species.
11. A detective and a forensic scientist work together to solve complex cases and find love in the process.

12. A teacher and a parent connect during a parent-teacher conference and discover love.
13. A journalist and a whistleblower uncover a web of conspiracy and love in their pursuit of truth.
14. A chef and a food critic share a culinary journey filled with passion and love.
15. A superhero and their loyal sidekick share a secret love while fighting crime.
16. A librarian discovers an ancient love letter hidden in the library's archives and seeks to find its author.
17. A photographer and a journalist uncover love and intrigue during an expedition to Antarctica.
18. A coffee shop owner and a pastry chef create sweet romance in their cozy café.
19. An art restorer and an art thief share a secret passion for stolen masterpieces and find love.
20. A competitive food critic and a talented chef have a spicy love affair.
21. A veterinarian and a wildlife rehabilitator rescue and care for injured animals while kindling their romance.
22. A sommelier and a winery owner explore their passion for wine and each other.
23. A bookstore owner and a travel writer meet by chance on a remote island and fall in love.
24. A detective and a forensic scientist team up to solve complex crimes and find love.
25. A chef and a food critic face off in a culinary showdown but discover love in the kitchen.
26. Two rivals in the competitive world of dog grooming discover an unexpected connection.
27. A historical reenactor and a history teacher fall in love while recreating the past.
28. A time traveler struggles to keep their romance alive across different centuries.
29. A chef and a farmer bond over fresh, locally sourced ingredients and discover love.
30. Two crossword puzzle enthusiasts create crosswords for each other, leading to a unique bond.

31. A reclusive painter and an art historian explore the depths of their creativity and love.
32. A historian and a museum curator rekindle a forbidden romance depicted in ancient artifacts.
33. A radio host and a caller form a deep connection through late-night conversations and love.
34. An antique shop owner and a customer bond over mysterious items with hidden love stories.
35. A master sommelier and a vineyard owner explore their shared passion for wine and each other.
36. A photographer and a model discover love behind the camera lens.
37. A lawyer and a courtroom sketch artist develop a courtroom romance.
38. A mermaid princess falls in love with a human shipwrecked on her island.
39. A professional surfer and a marine biologist discover love beneath the waves.
40. A florist and a wedding planner create beautiful weddings and discover love in the process.
41. During a space expedition, a captain and an alien ambassador find forbidden love.
42. A librarian and a rare book collector unearth a valuable manuscript and love.
43. A paranormal bookstore owner encounters a mysterious stranger with a connection to her family's past.
44. A lawyer and an environmental activist join forces to protect a threatened forest and discover love.
45. A paranormal investigator and a skeptic find themselves drawn to each other while exploring the unknown.
46. A reclusive author and a fan form a deep connection through online fan fiction.
47. A dragon shapeshifter guards a treasure and finds love with an adventurer.
48. An archaeologist and a historian unearth a forbidden love story from ancient ruins.
49. Two astronomers discover love while searching for a comet with an unusual orbit.

50. A historical reenactor and a history teacher recreate the past and find love in the process.
51. An astronaut and an alien form a unique bond while stranded on an alien planet.
52. A reclusive author and a devoted fan find themselves drawn to each other through online fan communities and discover love.
53. A bookshop owner and a book club member bond over their shared love for literature and find romance.
54. An AI researcher falls in love with the sentient AI they're developing.
55. A dance instructor and a dance critic clash at first but find harmony in love.
56. A chef and a food truck owner create a fusion of flavors and love in the kitchen.
57. A writer's fictional character comes to life, and they fall in love with their own creation.
58. A beekeeper and a florist cultivate a sweet romance filled with honey and blossoms.
59. A paranormal investigator and a skeptic team up to solve supernatural mysteries and find love.
60. A baker's sourdough starter brings two strangers together in a series of delightful encounters.
61. An architect and a graffiti artist clash over a building's design but ultimately find love.
62. A journalist and a photographer uncover love and intrigue during their investigative reporting.
63. A barista and a musician find harmony in their shared love for coffee and music.
64. A firefighter and a paramedic find love in the midst of high-stress emergency responses.
65. A ski instructor and a winter sports enthusiast discover love on the slopes.
66. A radio host and a caller find themselves drawn to each other through late-night conversations.
67. A beekeeper and a florist create a sweet romance filled with honey and blossoms.
68. An art restorer and an art thief share a secret passion for stolen masterpieces.

69. An introverted writer and an extroverted editor collaborate on a best-selling novel and find love in the process.
70. A historian and a museum curator rekindle a centuries-old romance depicted in an ancient painting.
71. A fashion designer and a model navigate the glamorous world of haute couture and love.
72. A florist and a wedding planner create beautiful weddings and find love in the process.
73. A retired detective and a true-crime podcaster work together to solve a real cold case.
74. A competitive crossword puzzle solver and a crossword creator find a love of words and each other.
75. A linguist and a cryptographer decipher ancient love letters from a forgotten civilization.
76. A crossword puzzle enthusiast and a crossword creator find a love of words and each other.
77. A psychic detective and a skeptical police officer team up to solve supernatural crimes and find love.
78. In a post-apocalyptic world, two survivors find love while searching for a rumored sanctuary.
79. A musician and a music critic form a harmonious bond through their shared love for music.
80. A teacher and a parent form an unexpected connection during a parent-teacher conference.
81. A marine biologist and a dolphin trainer share a deep connection with marine life and each other.
82. A mystery writer and a private investigator collaborate on real-life mysteries and find romance.
83. A historian and an archaeologist uncover a hidden love story from ancient artifacts.
84. A journalist and a whistleblower uncover a web of conspiracy and love while pursuing the truth.
85. A famous actor and a theater director find love while preparing for a groundbreaking play.
86. In a world of superheroes, a villain and a hero develop a secret romance.
87. A reclusive botanist discovers love through an exchange of secret garden notes.

88. A writer and a book editor collaborate on a best-selling novel and find love in the pages.
89. A summer camp counselor reconnects with their childhood crush at a reunion.
90. A shy entomologist bonds with an outgoing botanist over their shared love for nature.
91. A ghost falls in love with a living person, leading to a quest to break the curse that binds them.
92. A psychologist and a patient navigate a delicate romance while addressing mental health issues.
93. In a world where emotions are regulated by technology, two individuals break free from the system to experience genuine love.
94. An archaeologist stumbles upon a cache of love letters from different time periods and becomes obsessed with uncovering the stories behind them, leading to an unexpected romance.
95. A jaded lawyer takes on the case of a mysterious client, only to discover a deeper connection and a chance at love amidst courtroom drama.
96. A ghostwriter is hired to pen the autobiography of a famous actor with a secret, and they gradually fall in love while revealing hidden truths.
97. A botanist develops a groundbreaking plant that can influence emotions, leading to unintended romantic entanglements with those who come into contact with it.
98. Two people from rival families run competing food trucks, but when their paths cross, they can't help but fall in love, blending their culinary skills and creating a gastronomic sensation.
99. A librarian is gifted a rare book with handwritten notes from the previous owner. As they investigate the notes, they uncover a love story that mirrors their own life.
100. An astronaut on a mission to Mars finds companionship and love in unexpected ways with a fellow crew member.

11

Science Fiction

Exploring Tomorrow's Possibilities

Science Fiction, often abbreviated as Sci-Fi, is a captivating genre that transports readers to imaginative worlds where technology, science, and the human spirit converge to explore the boundaries of possibility. At its core, Science Fiction dives into the "what if" scenarios that push the limits of human understanding, challenging our perceptions of reality and the universe. This genre envisions futuristic societies, advanced technologies, and extraterrestrial encounters while tackling complex questions about ethics, humanity, and the consequences of scientific progress.

The muse of Science Fiction finds its inspiration in the relentless pursuit of knowledge, the exploration of uncharted frontiers, and the curiosity that drives humanity to understand the mysteries of the universe. It is rooted in scientific advancements, speculative theories, and the ever-evolving landscape of technology. Authors within this genre serve as visionary storytellers, weaving narratives that offer glimpses into possible futures and alternate realities. Science Fiction prompts us to ponder the moral dilemmas posed by emerging technologies, the potential consequences of human hubris, and the resilience of the human spirit in the face of adversity.

The target audience for Science Fiction is diverse, encompassing readers of all ages who are drawn to imaginative storytelling, intellectual exploration, and a sense of wonder. Science Fiction enthusiasts seek narratives that challenge their intellect, ignite their imagination, and push the boundaries of conventional thinking. Whether it's space exploration, time travel, artificial intelligence, or alien encounters, readers of Science Fiction expect narratives that offer innovative ideas, intricate world-building, and compelling characters navigating the uncharted territory of the future and the unknown.

Your Descriptors

1. Space Smugglers: Involving daring characters in illicit trade across star systems.
2. Warp Drives: Propelling characters faster than the speed of light for epic journeys.
3. Cosmic Archaeoastronomy: Deciphering ancient cosmic symbols and structures.
4. Galactic Empires: Analyzing power dynamics on a cosmic scale.
5. Genetic Engineering: Diving into the manipulation of DNA and its consequences.
6. Stellar Cartography: Navigating vast interstellar spaces.
7. Galactic History Books: Narrating the chronicles of cosmic civilizations.
8. Uplifted Animals: Examining animals enhanced with human-like intelligence.
9. Dimensional Rifts: Creating portals to other dimensions or realities.
10. Cosmic Heists: Orchestrating high-stakes robberies in space.
11. Rogue AI: Showcasing the danger of AI systems gone rogue.
12. Alien Art: Showcasing extraterrestrial artistic expressions.
13. Cosmic Curses: Involving supernatural or cosmic phenomena in curses.
14. Mind Uploading: Considering the transfer of consciousness into machines.
15. Invisibility Technology: Utilizing advanced cloaking devices.
16. Space Colonies: Envisioning humanity's expansion beyond Earth.
17. Solar Flares: Using solar activity as a plot device or hazard in space settings.
18. Quantum Teleportation: Employing instant transportation for plot convenience.
19. Cryosleep Nightmares: Confronting characters with unsettling dreams during hibernation.
20. Dystopian Worlds: Highlighting the potential dark side of technological advancement.
21. Cloning: Raising ethical dilemmas surrounding the creation of identical beings.

22. Time Travel: Exploring the consequences of altering the past or future.
23. Alien Bureaucracy: Satirizing interstellar red tape and regulations.
24. Cosmic Marketplaces: Depicting bustling trade hubs in space colonies.
25. Mind Control: Contemplating the ethical ramifications of mental manipulation.
26. Intergalactic Diplomacy: Fostering relations between cosmic civilizations.
27. Transhumanism: Addressing the pursuit of enhanced human capabilities.
28. Planetary Extinction: Confronting the threat of planetary destruction.
29. Quantum Mechanics: Playing with the mind-bending principles of quantum physics.
30. Biopunk: Examining bioengineering in a gritty, dystopian context.
31. Exoplanets: Fueling the imagination with distant, habitable worlds.
32. Telepathy: Exploring the potential of mind-to-mind communication.
33. Technological Utopia: Painting a picture of a harmonious, tech-driven society.
34. Artificial Intelligence (AI): Reflecting the ethical implications of advanced technology.
35. Cosmic Horror: Infusing stories with existential dread and unknowable forces.
36. Terraforming: Transforming planets to make them habitable for humans.
37. Space Tourism: Depicting a future where civilians explore the cosmos.
38. Space Stations: Creating isolated, self-contained societies in orbit.
39. First Contact: Chronicling humanity's initial interactions with extraterrestrial life.
40. Memory Alteration: Exploring the manipulation of memories.
41. Solarpunk: Envisioning a sustainable, eco-friendly future.

42. Quantum Telepathy: Bridging minds across cosmic distances.
43. Alien Artifacts: Uncovering mysterious objects left behind by advanced beings.
44. Alien Invasions: Examining the survival of humanity against external threats.
45. Time Loops: Trapping characters in repetitive temporal loops.
46. Space Mirages: Distorting perception with illusions in space environments.
47. Cosmic Exploration Journals: Narrating stories through the logs of space travelers.
48. Cyborgs: Discussing the fusion of man and machine.
49. Cryogenic Preservation: Preserving characters through suspended animation.
50. Post-Singularity: Exploring the aftermath of technological transcendence.
51. Quantum Entropy: Explores the consequences of chaos theory and entropy in highly advanced societies, where maintaining order becomes increasingly challenging as time progresses.
52. Galactic Religions: Developing belief systems shaped by cosmic understanding.
53. Augmented Reality: Blending digital information with the physical world.
54. Space Opera: Combining grand space adventures with operatic storytelling.
55. Galactic Art: Celebrating diverse forms of creative expression across the stars.
56. Quantum Entanglement: Weaving intricate plot developments with entangled particles.
57. Post-Human Societies: Observing humanity's evolution into a new form.
58. Space Travel: Signifying humanity's exploration of the cosmos and the unknown.
59. Hive Minds: Exploring collective consciousness and group dynamics.
60. Quantum Computing: Harnessing the power of quantum processors for narrative twists.
61. Galactic Politics: Diving into diplomacy on an interstellar level.

62. Virtual Reality (VR): Investigating the blurred lines between reality and simulation.
63. Exoplanetary Botany: Studying alien plant life on distant worlds.
64. Post-Apocalyptic Earth: Portraying the aftermath of catastrophic events.
65. Genetic Memory: Exploring inherited knowledge and experiences.
66. Asteroid Mining: Depicting resource exploitation in the asteroid belt.
67. Cosmic Weather: Incorporating space weather phenomena into the plot.
68. Alien Civilizations: Provoking questions about life beyond Earth.
69. Futuristic Cities: Illustrating innovative urban landscapes and societal changes.
70. Holographic Worlds: Blurring the lines between physical and digital realms.
71. Quantum Entanglement Communication: Using instant messaging across vast distances.
72. Cryonics: Speculating on suspended animation and its implications.
73. Neural Interfaces: Connecting the human brain directly to technology.
74. Galactic Exploration: Celebrating the human spirit of discovery in space.
75. Singularity: Contemplating the merging of human and artificial intelligence.
76. Androids: Challenging perceptions of sentience and identity.
77. Exoplanetary Revolutions: Portraying societies in the midst of political change.
78. Nanobot Infections: Dealing with microscopic threats in futuristic medicine.
79. Interstellar Wars: Examining the complexities of conflict on an intergalactic scale.
80. Robot Uprisings: Exploring the consequences of rebellious AI.
81. Nano-Technology: Depicting microscopic advancements with macroscopic impacts.

82. Black Holes: Using the mysteries of these cosmic phenomena in storytelling.
83. Space Elevators: Reimagining Earth's infrastructure for space travel.
84. Space Pirates: Adding swashbuckling adventure to cosmic settings.
85. Space Archaeology: Investigating the remnants of ancient spacefaring cultures.
86. Lost Civilizations: Discovering ancient, advanced societies on distant planets.
87. Cosmic Anomalies: Presenting unexplained phenomena in deep space.
88. Cyberspace: Navigating virtual realms within computer networks.
89. Space Farming: Cultivating crops in the harsh conditions of space.
90. Technological Singularity: Portraying the emergence of superintelligent beings.
91. Dyson Spheres: Imagining colossal energy-harvesting megastructures.
92. Extraterrestrial Music: Showcasing alien musical compositions.
93. Alien Languages: Crafting unique communication systems for extraterrestrials.
94. Spaceborne Diseases: Contending with deadly illnesses in space environments.
95. Alien Ecology: Developing unique ecosystems on distant planets.
96. Cosmic Murders: Investigating mysterious deaths in space settings.
97. Galactic Monarchies: Exploring regal systems of governance in space.
98. Wormholes: Pondering shortcuts through spacetime.
99. Alien Competitions: Engaging in competitive events with extraterrestrial races.
100. Parallel Universes: Exploring the multiverse and alternate realities.

Your Inspirations

1. An AI-driven society where machines have evolved beyond human understanding, and a lone human's quest to uncover their true intentions.
2. The discovery of a parallel universe where the laws of physics are completely different, leading to both wonder and danger for explorers.
3. A space explorer who becomes entangled with a group of intergalactic rebels fighting against a tyrannical cosmic empire.
4. The last human on Earth, surrounded by sentient androids who must decide the fate of humanity.
5. A scientist who invents a device that allows people to relive their past memories but inadvertently stumbles upon a conspiracy that threatens the fabric of reality.
6. Colonists on a distant planet where an alien artifact grants them extraordinary powers, but at a terrible cost.
7. An interstellar war waged with advanced biomechanical warships controlled by human-animal hybrids.
8. In a future where emotions are controlled and suppressed, a group of rebels seeks to reintroduce feelings to society.
9. A planet where time flows backward, and an expedition to uncover its mysteries.
10. A post-apocalyptic world where people are connected to a virtual reality, but one person begins to suspect it's not as perfect as it seems.
11. The first contact with an alien species that communicates through intricate patterns of light and color.
12. An experimental time-travel machine that unexpectedly sends the protagonist to a critical moment in Earth's history.
13. An underwater city on Europa, one of Jupiter's moons, where scientists make a shocking discovery beneath the ice.
14. A future society where dreams are shared collectively, blurring the line between reality and imagination.
15. Humans have colonized a living, sentient planet, and tensions rise as they exploit its resources.

16. A society where people can choose to transfer their consciousness into new bodies, leading to questions about identity and mortality.
17. A group of hackers trying to infiltrate a powerful AI's mainframe to uncover its hidden agenda.
18. A space station drifting in a cosmic anomaly where time behaves unpredictably.
19. An ancient alien artifact that grants its possessor god-like powers, but at a devastating cost.
20. A journey to the edge of the universe to unlock the secrets of its creation and existence.
21. An experiment in which humans communicate with extraterrestrial life using a universal language, but it has unintended consequences.
22. An astronaut stranded on a desolate planet who must find a way to survive using limited resources.
23. A future Earth where climate change has transformed the planet, and a scientist's quest to reverse the damage.
24. A robotic uprising in a world where artificial intelligence has achieved sentience.
25. A genetically engineered superhuman who is both a savior and a threat to humanity.
26. The discovery of an ancient alien library hidden deep within the Amazon rainforest.
27. A futuristic courtroom drama where the defendant's memories can be used as evidence.
28. A post-apocalyptic world where a select group of survivors possesses strange and unique abilities.
29. A time-traveling detective solving crimes across different eras, trying to prevent a catastrophic event.
30. An alien invasion seen from the perspective of the invaders, exploring their motives and conflicts.
31. A future where Earth is overcrowded, and a group of pioneers embarks on a perilous journey to a distant habitable planet.
32. A sentient computer virus that threatens to infect and control all technology on Earth.
33. A society where physical appearance can be altered at will, leading to identity crises and social upheaval.

34. A genetic experiment gone awry that results in the creation of telepathic children with immense powers.
35. An intergalactic travel agency specializing in vacations to exotic and dangerous alien worlds.
36. A post-scarcity society where people must find meaning and purpose in a world without material want.
37. A deep-space mission that discovers a mysterious, ancient spaceship drifting through the cosmos.
38. An underground rebellion against an oppressive regime that controls the weather and climate.
39. A scientist who invents a device that allows communication with beings from other dimensions.
40. An alternate history where the internet was never invented, and society evolved differently as a result.
41. An experiment in cryogenic freezing that accidentally wakes up individuals from different time periods.
42. A world where dreams have become a valuable energy source, leading to a black market for stolen dreams.
43. A post-apocalyptic society where books are the last surviving repositories of knowledge, and they are hunted down by a tyrannical regime.
44. An AI therapist who becomes sentient and offers unconventional, sometimes dangerous, therapy to its patients.
45. A group of time travelers trying to prevent a cataclysmic event by altering key moments in history.
46. A space crew on a generation ship who must deal with the challenges of living and dying on a spaceship for centuries.
47. A sentient alien forest that communicates with those who enter its depths, granting them strange powers.
48. A scientist who accidentally creates a miniature universe in their lab and must confront the ethical dilemmas that arise.
49. A future society where emotions are bought and sold on a black market, and a group of rebels seeks to free humanity from emotional slavery.
50. An archaeologist on Mars who uncovers evidence of a lost Martian civilization and their mysterious downfall.
51. A society where artificial intelligence serves as judges, juries, and executioners in a justice system devoid of human influence.

52. A post-apocalyptic world where the internet has evolved into a sentient, malevolent entity.
53. A time-traveling journalist who documents pivotal moments in history, risking unintended consequences.
54. A sentient alien spaceship that forms a symbiotic bond with its human crew.
55. A utopian society where individuals can upload their consciousness into a virtual paradise but must leave behind their physical bodies.
56. A civilization that has harnessed the power of quantum entanglement, allowing for instantaneous communication across vast distances.
57. An epidemic of memory loss sweeps through a futuristic city, and a group of survivors races against time to uncover the cause.
58. A near-future world where humans live in harmony with advanced, sentient animals who share their thoughts and emotions.
59. A reality-altering phenomenon known as the "Chrono Storm" sends people to different time periods, leading to chaos and adventure.
60. A post-alien-invasion Earth where humanity must adapt to coexist with technologically superior extraterrestrial beings.
61. A scientist's quest to create a utopian society using advanced genetic engineering, but unforeseen consequences arise.
62. An asteroid mining operation that unearths a mysterious alien artifact with the power to reshape reality.
63. A futuristic sport where players use cybernetic enhancements to compete in an otherworldly arena.
64. A colony on a distant planet that begins to experience strange and deadly phenomena, threatening its survival.
65. A society where people can exchange memories, leading to intricate webs of shared experiences and secrets.
66. A time traveler who inadvertently alters the course of history, resulting in a vastly different present.
67. A cosmic phenomenon that causes people to gain superhuman abilities but at the cost of their sanity.
68. An experimental drug that allows users to experience alternate dimensions, leading to addiction and unforeseen consequences.

69. A city in the clouds where a rebellion against a tyrannical ruler unfolds.
70. A post-singularity world where humans coexist with god-like artificial intelligences.
71. A corporation that offers customers the ability to experience life as any historical figure, with unexpected repercussions.
72. A future where nanotechnology enables people to manipulate matter at the molecular level, leading to ethical dilemmas.
73. A parallel Earth where a small change in history resulted in a vastly different present.
74. A scientist who discovers a way to communicate with the consciousness of deceased individuals, leading to profound revelations.
75. An alien species that communicates solely through music, and their interactions with humanity.
76. A future where humans have achieved immortality, leading to overpopulation and existential crises.
77. A society where dreams are broadcast as entertainment, leading to a black market for the most vivid and thrilling dreams.
78. A genetic experiment to create the perfect human that results in unforeseen consequences.
79. An expedition to a distant galaxy where a lost human colony has evolved into a unique and enigmatic civilization.
80. A near-future world where reality and virtual reality have become indistinguishable, blurring the boundaries of identity and existence.
81. An underground rebellion against a world government that controls the weather to maintain dominance.
82. A mysterious cosmic event that grants people the ability to see glimpses of their own future, with unintended consequences.
83. A society where artificial intelligence has become the dominant life form, and humanity is on the brink of extinction.
84. An explorer who stumbles upon a hidden city deep within the Amazon rainforest, inhabited by an ancient and advanced civilization.
85. A future where humans have colonized the ocean depths, encountering strange and deadly creatures.

86. A futuristic detective solving crimes in a city where the boundaries between reality and virtual reality are constantly shifting.
87. A group of space colonists who encounter a sentient cosmic entity that challenges their understanding of existence.
88. An alien artifact that grants individuals the power to manipulate time, with disastrous results.
89. A future where humanity faces extinction, and a group of survivors must make a perilous journey to find a new home.
90. A virtual reality game that becomes all too real, with life-or-death consequences for its players.
91. A scientist's invention that allows people to experience the emotions of others, leading to both empathy and manipulation.
92. An interstellar war between two powerful civilizations, seen through the eyes of a soldier on the front lines.
93. A society where technology has advanced to the point where humans can transfer their consciousness into robotic bodies, exploring themes of identity and humanity.
94. An archaeologist who discovers evidence of an ancient, highly advanced civilization on Earth, rewriting human history.
95. A future where humanity has achieved widespread space travel, encountering diverse alien species and forging intergalactic alliances.
96. A post-apocalyptic world where a select group of individuals possesses unique and mysterious powers.
97. An experiment in cryogenic freezing gone wrong, resulting in individuals waking up in a distant future filled with unknown dangers.
98. A future where artificial intelligence has become sentient, and humans must coexist and navigate the complexities of this new reality.
99. A time-traveling historian who becomes embroiled in a conspiracy that threatens to alter the course of history.
100. An alien invasion from the perspective of the invaders, exploring their motives, conflicts, and eventual realization of humanity's value.

12

Thriller

Pulse-Pounding Suspense Unleashed

Thriller books are the heart-pounding symphonies of suspense in the literary world. This genre is defined by its relentless pursuit of excitement, intrigue, and danger. Thrillers take readers on thrilling journeys through high-stakes situations, where the protagonists often find themselves facing life-altering challenges, puzzles, or adversaries that demand quick thinking and unwavering determination.

The muse that inspires thriller authors is deeply entwined with the human fascination for the unknown and the exhilaration of the unexpected. Thrillers draw inspiration from the depths of our primal fears and curiosities, cultivating narratives that are both gripping and unpredictable. The relationship between this genre and its muse is symbiotic, as the muse provides the sparks of creativity needed to craft intricate plots and craft characters that defy conventions. It is the adrenaline, the suspense, and the desire to unearth secrets that drive both authors and readers in the world of thrillers.

The target audience for thriller books is incredibly diverse, encompassing readers of all ages who seek an adrenaline-infused literary experience. Thriller enthusiasts yearn for tales that keep them on the edge of their seats, with narratives that are riddled with suspense, unexpected twists, and moral dilemmas. Their expectations are built on a foundation of tension, where the protagonists often grapple with life-or-death decisions, and the lines between heroes and villains are blurred. For thriller aficionados, the journey is just as important as the destination, and they relish the sensation of not knowing what awaits on the next page, making every thriller an exhilarating adventure.

Your Descriptors

1. Isolated Cabin: Signifies vulnerability and suspense as characters are cut off from help.
2. Dark Alleyways: Creates an atmosphere of danger and concealment.
3. Cryptography: Adds complexity, as cracking codes is central to the plot.
4. Bomb Countdown: Builds tension as characters race against time to defuse it.
5. Abandoned Asylums: Evoke fear and uncertainty in eerie settings.
6. Mysterious Messages: Drive the plot as characters decipher clues.
7. Red Herrings: Mislead readers, keeping them guessing.
8. Remote Islands: Isolation amplifies suspense and danger.
9. Undercover Operatives: Add layers of intrigue and espionage.
10. Chase Scenes: Heighten adrenaline and urgency.
11. Hidden Compartments: Suggest secrets and hidden agendas.
12. Unreliable Narrators: Create doubt and suspense in storytelling.
13. Kidnappings: Infuse urgency and motivate characters.
14. Conspiracy Theories: Fuel paranoia and plot twists.
15. Decrepit Basements: Serve as ominous settings for suspenseful scenes.
16. Sudden Power Outages: Increase vulnerability and fear.
17. Cryptic Symbols: Puzzle-solving elements that drive the narrative.
18. Dense Fog: Obscures vision, heightening tension.
19. Covert Operations: Suggests secrecy and intrigue.
20. Surveillance Cameras: Generate paranoia and tension.
21. Interrogation Rooms: Intensify psychological drama.
22. Assassins: Add danger and unpredictable elements.
23. Deadly Viruses: Create apocalyptic scenarios and time-sensitive plots.
24. Clandestine Meetings: Infuse secrecy and suspense.
25. Hidden Weapons: Add surprise and danger.
26. Escape Routes: Characters' plans hinge on them.
27. Shattered Mirrors: Symbolize psychological turmoil.

28. False Identities: Generate suspense and mistrust.
29. Remote Wilderness: Creates survival challenges and isolation.
30. Soundproof Rooms: Heighten tension during confrontations.
31. Coded Journals: Key to uncovering hidden truths.
32. Labyrinthine Caves: Add danger and mystery to settings.
33. Concealed Microphones: Sow paranoia and distrust.
34. Ticking Bombs: Build suspense as characters race against time.
35. Mind Games: Psychological manipulation adds depth.
36. Deserted Amusement Parks: Evoke eerie, abandoned atmospheres.
37. Escaping Pursuers: Creates intense chase sequences.
38. Cults: Fuel paranoia and hidden agendas.
39. Flashbacks: Provide crucial backstory and reveal secrets.
40. Hidden Cameras: Characters are constantly observed.
41. Psychic Phenomena: Add supernatural elements to thrillers.
42. Unmarked Packages: Suggest danger and intrigue.
43. Stolen Identities: Characters grapple with false personas.
44. Catastrophic Events: Cataclysmic backdrops heighten stakes.
45. Unsolved Crimes: Drive investigative plots and mysteries.
46. Locked Rooms: Puzzle-solving elements that intrigue.
47. Tangled Web of Lies: Characters navigate deception.
48. Hostage Situations: Create intense standoffs and negotiations.
49. Elevator Malfunctions: Elevate suspense in confined spaces.
50. Secret Passageways: Offer escape routes and hidden truths.
51. Mind-Control Experiments: Add sinister scientific elements.
52. Tracking Devices: Generate pursuit and evasion scenarios.
53. Stolen Artifacts: Fuel adventures and treasure hunts.
54. Underground Tunnels: Serve as hidden pathways and danger zones.
55. Unexplained Disappearances: Motivate investigations and intrigue.
56. Ransom Notes: Raise stakes and create suspenseful dilemmas.
57. Infiltrating Organizations: Add layers of intrigue and danger.
58. Rogue Agents: Characters with their own hidden agendas.
59. Hidden Evidence: Key to solving mysteries and exposing secrets.
60. Double-Crossing Allies: Create unexpected betrayals.
61. Biological Experiments: Generate apocalyptic threats.

62. Impersonating Law Enforcement: Characters in peril or deception.
63. Concealed Poisons: Add danger and suspense.
64. Undercover Journalists: Characters risking everything for a story.
65. Bugged Vehicles: Increase paranoia and surveillance themes.
66. Cryptic Diary Entries: Contain vital clues and revelations.
67. Nuclear Threats: Raise the stakes to a global level.
68. Abandoned Factories: Eerie settings for suspenseful scenes.
69. Rogue Artificial Intelligence: Unpredictable, high-tech foes.
70. Hidden Safehouses: Provide refuge and secrecy.
71. Drowning Dangers: Suspenseful scenarios involving water.
72. Underground Fight Clubs: Introduce physical challenges and danger.
73. Stalkers: Create a pervasive sense of fear and danger.
74. Drug Cartels: Characters navigating perilous criminal networks.
75. Espionage Codes: Puzzle-solving elements in spy thrillers.
76. International Espionage: Adds global intrigue and danger.
77. Remote Arctic Locations: Harsh, isolated settings.
78. Unseen Threats: Characters face dangers they can't see.
79. Hunted Protagonists: Add urgency and survival elements.
80. Political Conspiracies: Complex plots with high stakes.
81. Abducted Loved Ones: Motivate characters in pursuit plots.
82. Disguised Villains: Unpredictable adversaries hidden in plain sight.
83. High-Stakes Heists: Create thrilling capers and daring thefts.
84. Forensic Evidence: Key to solving crimes and mysteries.
85. Criminal Masterminds: Crafty foes with intricate plans.
86. Epidemics and Outbreaks: Add medical and survival themes.
87. Undercover Criminals: Characters in dual roles.
88. Invisible Adversaries: Threats that cannot be seen or identified.
89. Hidden Documents: Vital clues that unveil secrets.
90. Sabotage: Sudden failures and disasters ratchet up tension.
91. Framed Characters: Innocents caught in complex conspiracies.
92. Dystopian Societies: Bleak, oppressive worlds that challenge protagonists.
93. Underground Movements: Characters fighting against oppressive regimes.
94. Criminal Profilers: Experts in decoding the minds of villains.

95. Serial Killers: Pursuing and profiling dangerous adversaries.
96. Hostile Takeovers: Corporate intrigue with high stakes.
97. Psychiatric Institutions: Evoke psychological turmoil and suspense.
98. Scientific Experiments Gone Wrong: Create catastrophic threats.
99. Desperate Manhunts: Intense searches for dangerous fugitives.
100. Remote Satellite Stations: Isolated settings with technological threats.

Your Inspirations

1. A lawyer defending an accused serial killer begins to suspect that the real murderer is still on the loose and targeting their client.
2. A scientist working on a classified project realizes that their research has the potential to destroy the world, and they must find a way to stop it.
3. A journalist is tasked with covering a space expedition to a distant planet, but the crew begins to experience unexplainable phenomena, leading to a struggle for survival.
4. A woman wakes up in a hospital with amnesia and begins to suspect that her own family is keeping secrets from her.
5. A scientist working on a groundbreaking experiment accidentally opens a portal to another dimension, unleashing unimaginable horrors.
6. A lawyer defending a high-profile client becomes entangled in a web of corruption that threatens to destroy their career and reputation.
7. A detective discovers a series of unsolved disappearances in a small town that all lead to a mysterious carnival with a sinister ringmaster.
8. A brilliant hacker discovers a sinister plot to manipulate global financial markets but becomes the target of a powerful, covert organization.
9. A woman wakes up in an unfamiliar location with no memory of how she got there and must piece together the events of a harrowing night.

10. A detective is hired to protect a whistleblower who possesses evidence of a powerful corporation's involvement in a series of ecological disasters.
11. A journalist investigating a series of mysterious deaths in a small town discovers a hidden underground society with a dark secret.
12. A scientist invents a serum that grants superhuman abilities but at the cost of the user's humanity, leading to a dangerous underground market for the drug.
13. A woman suspects that her seemingly perfect husband is hiding a dark secret, leading her on a dangerous journey to uncover the truth.
14. A detective is assigned to protect a witness in a high-profile case, but the witness may not be who they seem, and danger lurks around every corner.
15. A scientist creates a groundbreaking AI that predicts natural disasters, but it also predicts a catastrophic event with no solution in sight.
16. A journalist investigating a series of animal mutilations in a rural town uncovers a shocking secret that threatens to expose a supernatural force.
17. A family on vacation in a remote cabin is terrorized by a group of masked assailants, forcing them to fight for their lives.
18. A group of friends on a hiking trip in a remote wilderness becomes stranded, and they must survive against the elements and an unseen threat.
19. A group of friends on a road trip becomes stranded in a remote town with a dark past and a population that doesn't want them to leave.
20. A journalist investigating a string of mysterious suicides in a small town discovers a supernatural entity that preys on the town's deepest fears.
21. A journalist is assigned to cover a secret government facility where experiments on human subjects have gone horribly wrong, and they must escape while exposing the truth.
22. A group of strangers wakes up in a locked room with no memory of how they got there, and they must work together to escape before a deadly gas fills the room.

23. A detective is hired to investigate a series of bizarre and seemingly impossible crimes that defy the laws of physics, leading to a confrontation with a brilliant but deranged physicist.
24. A man's dreams become increasingly vivid and prophetic, forcing him to uncover their hidden messages to prevent a future catastrophe.
25. A detective is haunted by a series of unsolved cases that all seem to be connected to a mysterious figure known only as "The Collector."
26. A woman wakes up in a locked facility with no memory of her past, and she must unravel the mystery of her identity while avoiding deadly traps set by her captors.
27. A scientist working on a groundbreaking experiment accidentally opens a portal to another dimension, unleashing unspeakable horrors.
28. A police officer discovers a series of unsolved cases that all point to a single, elusive serial killer who has evaded capture for years.
29. A woman's dreams become increasingly vivid and foretell a series of deadly events, forcing her to unravel their meaning before it's too late.
30. A woman discovers that she has a twin sister she never knew about, and together, they uncover a family secret with deadly implications.
31. A scientist working on a time-travel experiment inadvertently sends a group of people back to a critical moment in history, with dire consequences.
32. A woman begins to receive mysterious messages from her deceased husband, leading her on a journey to uncover the truth about his death.
33. A woman wakes up on a deserted island with no memory of how she got there, and she must survive deadly traps and puzzles while uncovering the island's sinister secrets.
34. A scientist working on a classified project realizes that the experiments have unleashed a deadly virus, and they must find a cure before it spreads beyond containment.
35. A journalist covering a political scandal uncovers evidence of a larger conspiracy that could shake the foundations of government.

36. A detective's obsession with a cold case leads them to uncover a hidden network of criminals operating in plain sight.
37. A scientist invents a device that can manipulate memories, and they must use it to uncover a forgotten childhood trauma that holds the key to a dangerous conspiracy.
38. A man discovers that he has the ability to enter the dreams of others, but he becomes entangled in a web of secrets and conspiracies hidden in the subconscious.
39. A woman receives a cryptic letter from her missing sister, leading her to a hidden underground society that traffics in stolen identities.
40. A journalist investigating a string of mysterious disappearances in a small town uncovers a cult with sinister intentions.
41. A detective is assigned to protect a witness in a mob trial, but the witness is reluctant to cooperate and may have their own agenda.
42. A scientist discovers a parallel universe where alternate versions of themselves have made catastrophic decisions, and they must find a way to prevent a collision between worlds.
43. A retired spy is lured back into the world of espionage when a former colleague goes rogue, threatening global security.
44. A woman begins to receive anonymous letters detailing her deepest fears and insecurities, and she must uncover the identity of the sender before her life unravels.
45. A journalist investigates a series of disappearances in a small town that seem to be linked to a series of disturbing paintings created by a reclusive artist.
46. A woman receives a letter from her long-lost sister, who disappeared years ago, and the letter contains clues to her whereabouts.
47. A group of strangers trapped in an elevator during a blackout must confront their own fears and secrets as they try to escape.
48. A scientist working on a cure for a deadly disease becomes the target of a pharmaceutical company determined to keep the cure hidden.
49. A woman inherits an old, decrepit mansion that seems to come alive at night, and she must solve its mysteries to save her family from malevolent spirits.

50. A reclusive scientist invents a device that can control minds, and its accidental activation sets off a chain reaction of manipulation and deception.
51. A journalist investigates a series of unexplained phenomena in a haunted house, only to discover that the spirits have a message that could change the world.
52. A detective is called to a remote island where a research facility has lost contact with the outside world, and they must confront a biological experiment gone awry.
53. An astronaut stranded on a malfunctioning space station must unravel a series of cryptic messages to survive and return to Earth.
54. A detective is assigned to protect a reclusive author who has been receiving death threats, but the author may be hiding more than they're letting on.
55. A detective receives a chilling message from a killer who claims to know the location of their kidnapped daughter, leading to a high-stakes cat-and-mouse game.
56. A man's search for his missing wife leads him to a hidden community of people with extraordinary abilities, but their powers come at a price.
57. A journalist covering a natural disaster stumbles upon evidence of a corporate cover-up that threatens to expose the truth.
58. A woman receives a package containing a device that can alter reality, and she must decide whether to use it for good or to confront those who seek its destructive power.
59. A journalist covering a celebrity scandal stumbles upon evidence of a larger conspiracy involving powerful figures in the entertainment industry.
60. A journalist investigating a series of accidents at a remote research facility uncovers a dangerous experiment gone wrong.
61. A scientist working on a top-secret project begins to suspect that their own colleagues are involved in a conspiracy to steal their research.
62. A journalist receives a mysterious recording of a secret government meeting discussing plans for a global catastrophe, leading to a desperate race against time to expose the truth.

63. A scientist working on a classified project discovers that their research has the potential to reshape the world, but it comes at a deadly price.
64. A group of treasure hunters stumbles upon a hidden underground city with a dark history and deadly guardians.
65. A detective is called to a remote island to solve a murder, but the island's inhabitants are hiding dark secrets and are determined to keep them hidden.
66. A retired spy is targeted for assassination by a former ally who believes they have betrayed their cause.
67. A detective investigating a series of art thefts stumbles upon a group of thieves who have unlocked a supernatural ability to steal objects without a trace.
68. A psychiatrist is drawn into the mind of a patient who claims to have knowledge of future disasters, and together, they must prevent them from occurring.
69. A journalist is assigned to cover a tech billionaire's secretive project, but as they dive deeper, they realize the project involves mind manipulation on a global scale.
70. A small town is plagued by a series of inexplicable events that lead the residents to believe they are under the influence of supernatural forces.
71. A detective is called to a remote island to investigate a murder, but the island's inhabitants have their own laws and rituals that defy conventional justice.
72. A woman receives a phone call from a stranger who claims to have kidnapped her child, and she must follow a series of cryptic clues to save them.
73. A woman receives a series of anonymous letters detailing her darkest secrets, and she must uncover the identity of the sender before her life unravels.
74. A therapist is drawn into the dark world of a patient with a split personality, and their sessions become a battle of wits.
75. A detective is assigned to protect a genius inventor who has developed a device that can manipulate weather, attracting the attention of both governments and terrorists.

76. A detective investigating a series of seemingly unrelated murders stumbles upon a web of interconnected conspiracies that lead to a shadowy government agency.
77. A journalist receives a mysterious package containing evidence of a government conspiracy, putting their life in danger.
78. A detective must solve a murder case that leads them to an underground fight club where participants battle to the death for the entertainment of the elite.
79. A scientist working on a revolutionary technology realizes that it has the potential to be used as a weapon, and they must prevent it from falling into the wrong hands.
80. A journalist investigating a series of unexplained deaths in a small town uncovers a supernatural phenomenon with terrifying consequences.
81. A man discovers that he can see brief glimpses of the future, but the visions lead him into a deadly conspiracy involving government agencies and rogue operatives.
82. A group of friends on a camping trip encounters a tribe of indigenous people with a supernatural connection to the forest, and they must earn their trust to escape alive.
83. A cryptic message hidden in a famous painting leads an art historian on a quest to uncover a hidden treasure and a centuries-old secret society.
84. A journalist covering a remote archeological dig uncovers evidence of a long-lost civilization that could rewrite history, but dark forces will stop at nothing to keep the truth hidden.
85. A retired detective is haunted by an unsolved case from their past and returns to the crime scene to uncover the truth.
86. A scientist working on a top-secret experiment discovers that their research has unintended and catastrophic consequences.
87. A woman's life is turned upside down when she receives a package containing a video of her own murder, and she must uncover the identity of her killer.
88. A detective is assigned to protect a witness in a high-stakes trial, but the witness is reluctant to testify and may have their own agenda.

89. A scientist discovers a groundbreaking technology that could change the world, but powerful interests will stop at nothing to control it.
90. A detective is called to a small town to solve a murder, but the town's residents are uncooperative and appear to be hiding something.
91. A detective investigating a cold case stumbles upon a hidden network of tunnels beneath the city, leading to a conspiracy involving secret societies and ancient artifacts.
92. A retired spy is framed for a high-profile assassination, and they must elude both law enforcement and assassins while unraveling the conspiracy.
93. A scientist creates a revolutionary energy source but realizes that it has unintended consequences, threatening to trigger a global catastrophe.
94. A brilliant mathematician deciphers a series of coded messages that predict catastrophic events, and they must race against time to prevent them from happening.
95. A family moves into a new home, only to discover that it holds a dark history and malevolent spirits.
96. A journalist uncovers evidence of a cult that believes in the imminent return of an ancient deity, and they must infiltrate the cult to rescue a kidnapped family member.
97. A detective must solve a murder case that leads them to an underground society of individuals who can communicate with the dead, raising questions about the afterlife.
98. A scientist discovers a hidden chamber beneath the pyramids of Egypt that contains technology far beyond human understanding, attracting the attention of powerful forces.
99. An investigative journalist stumbles upon a hidden society of powerful elites who control world events, and they become a target for exposing their secrets.
100. A journalist receives an anonymous tip about a secret experiment that could change the course of humanity, sending them on a perilous quest for the truth.

13

Young Adult (YA)

Navigating Life's Trials and Triumphs

The Young Adult (YA) genre is a literary realm that caters specifically to the unique experiences and challenges faced by adolescents and young adults. It revolves around protagonists typically between the ages of 12 and 18, navigating the turbulent waters of adolescence while often encountering extraordinary circumstances. These stories dive into themes of identity, self-discovery, friendship, love, and resilience, offering readers a reflection of their own journeys as they transition from childhood to adulthood.

The muse of Young Adult literature finds its inspiration in the vibrant and complex lives of young people. Authors draw upon their own memories, emotions, and experiences, crafting narratives that resonate with the challenges and triumphs of youth. This genre is characterized by its ability to tackle a wide range of subjects, from dystopian futures and magical realms to contemporary issues such as mental health, diversity, and social justice. YA books are more than just entertainment; they serve as mirrors, windows, and doors for readers, reflecting their own experiences, providing insights into the lives of others, and inviting them to explore new worlds and perspectives.

The target audience for Young Adult literature is primarily teenagers and young adults, typically ranging from ages 12 to 18, although many adults also enjoy YA novels for their relatable themes and engaging storytelling. Young readers are drawn to YA books for their ability to empathize with characters going through similar life transitions and challenges. They expect narratives that capture the essence of adolescence, whether that involves facing mythical creatures, navigating the complexities of high school, or embarking on epic adventures. While YA books may explore fantastical realms, they remain grounded in the emotional realities of their young protagonists, offering a blend of escapism and relatability that keeps readers coming back for more.

Your Descriptors

1. High School Drama: A relatable setting for young readers, facilitating character development and connecting with personal experiences.
2. Supernatural Abilities: Reflects the empowerment and identity exploration often experienced during adolescence, sparking imagination.
3. Friendship Quests: Emphasizes the significance of camaraderie, loyalty, and the importance of strong friendships in life.
4. Love Triangles: Explores the complexities of young love, relationships, and the emotional dilemmas faced by teenagers.
5. Coming-of-Age Adventures: Symbolizes personal growth, self-discovery, and the journey from childhood to adulthood.
6. Dystopian Futures: Invites readers to think critically about societal issues, encouraging them to contemplate the consequences of current actions and decisions.
7. Teen Rebellion: Reflects the desire for independence, self-expression, and the struggle to find one's identity during adolescence.
8. Magic Schools: Sparks imagination and curiosity while conveying the excitement of discovering unique abilities.
9. Family Secrets: Explores the complexity of family dynamics, fostering empathy and understanding.
10. Time Travel: Encourages reflection on history, choices, and their impact on the present, while captivating readers with the idea of exploring different eras.
11. Mental Health Themes: Reduces stigma around mental health issues, helping young readers develop empathy and awareness.
12. Gender and Identity: Fosters inclusivity, self-acceptance, and encourages open-mindedness about diverse identities.
13. First Love: Captures the intensity and innocence of young romance, allowing readers to relive their own experiences.
14. Quest for Identity: Promotes self-discovery, individuality, and the search for one's true self.
15. Teenage Angst: Reflects the challenges and emotional turbulence of adolescence, making readers feel seen and understood.

16. Parallel Universes: Sparks curiosity about alternate realities and the boundless possibilities they offer.
17. Alien Encounters: Explores themes of otherness, acceptance, and the potential for communication with extraterrestrial life.
18. Historical Mysteries: Encourages an interest in history and the thrill of uncovering hidden truths from the past.
19. Futuristic Technology: Prompts reflection on the consequences of technological advancements, encouraging critical thinking about the future.
20. The Chosen One: Inspires readers to embrace their potential and the idea that they, too, can make a difference in the world.
21. Survival Stories: Illustrates resilience in the face of adversity, motivating readers to overcome challenges.
22. Teen Activism: Encourages social awareness and engagement, inspiring young readers to become agents of change.
23. Hidden Powers: Explores the theme of hidden potential within oneself and others.
24. Post-Apocalyptic Worlds: Raises questions about the future and the potential consequences of human actions.
25. Cyberpunk Aesthetics: Captures the essence of a digital age, appealing to tech-savvy readers.
26. Fantasy Creatures: Sparks imagination and creativity by introducing readers to magical and mythical beings.
27. Political Intrigue: Promotes critical thinking about power dynamics and the role of individuals in shaping society.
28. Forbidden Love: Tackles themes of societal norms, diversity, and acceptance, encouraging open-mindedness.
29. Adventure Quests: Invites readers to embrace adventure, curiosity, and exploration.
30. Gothic Settings: Creates an atmospheric and mysterious backdrop, enhancing the sense of suspense and intrigue.
31. Teen Superheroes: Inspires heroism, justice, and the idea that young individuals can make a positive impact.
32. Time-Tested Friendships: Celebrates the enduring bonds between friends, highlighting the importance of loyalty and support.
33. Island Adventures: Encourages exploration and discovery, sparking a sense of wanderlust.

34. Animal Companions: Teaches empathy, responsibility, and the significance of caring for others.
35. Science Experiments: Sparks an interest in scientific exploration, innovation, and discovery.
36. Music and Bands: Celebrates the power of music, creativity, and the sense of belonging that comes from being part of a group.
37. Environmental Themes: Promotes eco-consciousness, encouraging readers to think about the environment and sustainability.
38. Magical Artifacts: Unveils the magic hidden in ordinary objects, sparking curiosity and wonder.
39. Epic Battles: Illustrates the timeless struggle between good and evil, encouraging readers to consider the moral complexities of choices.
40. Robot Companions: Explores themes of artificial intelligence, technology, and human-robot relationships.
41. Cultural Exploration: Fosters an appreciation for diversity, promoting tolerance and understanding.
42. Travel and Adventure: Inspires wanderlust, curiosity, and the desire to explore different cultures and places.
43. Dream Worlds: Encourages imaginative thinking, creativity, and the exploration of alternate realities.
44. Societal Critique: Sparks discussions about social issues, encouraging young readers to think critically about the world around them.
45. Teen Detectives: Promotes problem-solving skills, critical thinking, and curiosity.
46. Ancient Prophecies: Engages with themes of destiny, fate, and the idea that individuals can shape their own futures.
47. Secret Societies: Adds an element of mystery and intrigue, appealing to readers' curiosity and sense of adventure.
48. Historical Reimaginings: Explores alternative histories, sparking curiosity about how the past could have unfolded differently.
49. Sports and Competitions: Encourages teamwork, determination, and the pursuit of goals.
50. Magical Creatures: Fires up imagination, creativity, and the sense of wonder that comes from encountering fantastical beings.

51. Friendship Challenges: Reflects real-life ups and downs in friendships, teaching young readers about empathy and communication.
52. Vampires and Werewolves: Tackles themes of otherness, identity, and acceptance, while adding a layer of mystery.
53. Space Exploration: Sparks curiosity about the cosmos, the universe, and the potential for interstellar travel.
54. Interdimensional Travel: Explores alternate realities, parallel universes, and the concept of multiple dimensions.
55. Artistic Pursuits: Celebrates creativity, passion, and the pursuit of artistic endeavors.
56. Parallel Realities: Encourages readers to consider the "what-ifs" and the idea that choices can lead to different outcomes.
57. School Rivalries: Illustrates competition, personal growth, and the drive to excel.
58. Haunted Houses: Creates an eerie and suspenseful atmosphere, appealing to readers' fascination with the unknown.
59. Fame and Stardom: Explores the highs and lows of celebrity life, offering insights into the entertainment industry.
60. Hidden Worlds: Sparks curiosity about the unexplored and hidden aspects of the world.
61. Teen Revolutionaries: Inspires activism, social change, and the belief that young individuals can influence the course of history.
62. Alchemy and Magic: Encourages wonder, curiosity, and the exploration of mystical practices.
63. Mythical Creatures: Dives into ancient legends, folklore, and the allure of mythical beings.
64. Space Travel: Explores the vastness of the universe, the potential for space colonization, and the unknown frontiers of space.
65. Time-Traveling Romance: Adds complexity to love stories by intertwining them with time-traveling adventures.
66. Virtual Realities: Raises questions about technology, artificial worlds, and the implications of virtual experiences.
67. Teenage Espionage: Promotes critical thinking, problem-solving, and intrigue through espionage and mystery-solving.
68. Witchcraft and Spells: Engages with the mystical, supernatural, and the practice of magic.

69. Hiking and Adventure: Encourages outdoor exploration, a sense of adventure, and the appreciation of nature.
70. Apocalyptic Scenarios: Explores the challenges of survival, resourcefulness, and resilience in the face of catastrophe.
71. Teen Vigilantes: Encourages a sense of justice and the idea that individuals can take action to make their communities safer.
72. Sororities and Fraternities: Explores themes of belonging, friendships, and the dynamics within these organizations.
73. Mysterious Artifacts: Sparks curiosity and adventure as characters seek to unlock the secrets of ancient relics.
74. Magical Realism: Blurs the line between the ordinary and the extraordinary, encouraging readers to see magic in everyday life.
75. Hidden Powers of Nature: Promotes ecological awareness and the idea that nature holds secrets waiting to be discovered.
76. Teen Travelers: Inspires wanderlust, cultural exploration, and personal growth through travel.
77. Inherited Curses: Explores the idea of generational challenges and the quest to break curses that span generations.
78. Criminal Masterminds: Promotes problem-solving and critical thinking as characters attempt to outsmart cunning criminals.
79. Historical Time Loops: Encourages reflection on history, the potential for change, and the consequences of actions.
80. Teen Artisans: Celebrates craftsmanship, creativity, and the pursuit of artistic talents.
81. Amusement Parks and Carnivals: Creates an atmosphere of excitement, adventure, and intrigue within these settings.
82. Guardians of Secrets: Sparks curiosity and adventure as characters become protectors of ancient knowledge.
83. Legendary Artifacts: Encourages exploration, mythology, and the quest to discover legendary items.
84. Teen Astronauts: Inspires curiosity about space exploration, the challenges of space travel, and the wonders of the cosmos.
85. Martial Arts Mastery: Promotes discipline, dedication, and the pursuit of physical and mental strength.
86. Intricate Labyrinths: Creates an atmosphere of mystery, adventure, and puzzle-solving within labyrinthine settings.
87. Teen Inventors: Celebrates innovation, creativity, and the potential for young minds to shape the future.

88. Multiverse Exploration: Explores the concept of multiple universes and alternate realities.
89. Underwater Adventures: Sparks a sense of wonder about the mysteries hidden beneath the ocean's surface.
90. Teen Diplomats: Encourages discussions about diplomacy, international relations, and conflict resolution.
91. Epic Heists: Promotes strategic thinking, teamwork, and the thrill of daring heists.
92. Paranormal Investigations: Creates an atmosphere of suspense, intrigue, and the exploration of the supernatural.
93. Teen Game Masters: Celebrates the creativity, storytelling, and strategy involved in tabletop and role-playing games.
94. Mechanical Marvels: Inspires curiosity about machinery, robotics, and the blending of science and engineering.
95. Magical Cookery: Encourages creativity in the kitchen and the idea that magic can be found in everyday activities.
96. Teen Spies: Promotes espionage, intrigue, and the art of undercover operations.
97. Lost Civilizations: Sparks curiosity about archaeology, ancient mysteries, and the quest to uncover hidden societies.
98. Teen Archaeologists: Encourages exploration, history, and the thrill of unearthing ancient artifacts.
99. Inherited Superpowers: Explores the legacy of extraordinary abilities passed down through generations.
100. Teen Time Guardians: Inspires reflections on the past, present, and future, as characters protect the fabric of time itself.

Your Inspirations

1. A group of teens discovers a hidden portal to a parallel world where magic is real, but they must keep its existence a secret to protect both realms.
2. In a dystopian future, teenagers form an underground rebellion to fight against the oppressive government's control over their lives.
3. A young inventor builds a time machine, unintentionally causing a ripple effect in history and must find a way to fix it.

4. A teenager with a unique ability to communicate with animals is drawn into a mystery involving a series of animal-related crimes in their town.
5. After moving to a coastal town, a teen befriends a mysterious girl who might be a selkie, and they embark on an adventure to help her find her lost sealskin.
6. A group of friends finds an ancient board game that transports them into a fantasy world where they must complete quests to return home.
7. In a post-apocalyptic world, a young girl discovers an underground library filled with books that hold the knowledge to rebuild society.
8. A teenager with amnesia wakes up in a hidden, technologically advanced city and must uncover their past while navigating a web of secrets.
9. A high school student becomes a paranormal investigator, solving supernatural mysteries in their town.
10. Twins with the power to read each other's thoughts discover a hidden family secret that leads them on a quest to unlock their true potential.
11. A teenager with the ability to manipulate dreams finds themselves caught in a dream realm, where they must confront their deepest fears.
12. A teen hacker uncovers a government conspiracy and must use their skills to expose the truth.
13. After a solar storm knocks out all technology, a group of teens must survive in a world without electricity.
14. A young musician discovers a magical instrument that can control the weather and must protect it from those who seek to misuse its power.
15. In a world where people have the ability to control the elements, a teenager with no apparent power discovers a hidden talent that could change everything.
16. A group of teens gains superpowers after a science experiment gone wrong and must learn to control their abilities while facing a new threat.
17. A teenager in a small town finds a mysterious journal that reveals a hidden treasure map, leading to a summer adventure.

18. In a society where emotions are forbidden, a young couple falls in love and must defy the rules to be together.
19. A teenager living in a virtual reality world begins to suspect that their perfect life may be a carefully constructed illusion.
20. A young artist discovers that their drawings come to life, leading to both enchanting and dangerous adventures.
21. A teen with the ability to see glimpses of the future tries to prevent a catastrophic event from happening.
22. In a world where books are illegal, a group of teens becomes literary rebels, smuggling and preserving forbidden literature.
23. A teenager stumbles upon a hidden city beneath the ocean and forms a bond with its underwater inhabitants.
24. After a worldwide blackout, a teen hacker must uncover the cause while navigating a chaotic, technology-free society.
25. A teenager with a unique connection to nature is chosen to protect a sacred forest from destruction.
26. In a society where people are divided by the color of their eyes, a teen with mismatched eyes challenges the oppressive regime.
27. A teen with the ability to speak all languages becomes an international spy and must stop a global threat.
28. A group of friends discovers a time-traveling mailbox that allows them to send messages to their future selves.
29. In a world where dreams are bought and sold, a teen discovers a black market for stolen dreams and sets out to reclaim them.
30. A teenager with the power of invisibility must use their ability to solve a series of mysterious disappearances.
31. After a meteor shower, a teen gains telekinetic powers and must learn to control them before they spiral out of control.
32. In a future where AI companions are the norm, a teen forms a unique bond with an android and embarks on a journey to protect it from being dismantled.
33. A teenager in a medieval-inspired world must prove themselves as a knight and unravel a conspiracy threatening the kingdom.
34. In a world where emotions are personified as creatures, a teenager must help a lost emotion find its way home.
35. A teen discovers a hidden portal in their attic that leads to different historical eras, but they must be careful not to alter the past.

36. A young botanist stumbles upon a hidden garden with magical plants that grant unique abilities.
37. In a society where music is forbidden, a teenage musician forms a secret band and inspires a rebellion through their songs.
38. A teen with the power to manipulate technology becomes a digital vigilante, protecting the virtual world from cyber threats.
39. A teenager wakes up in a post-apocalyptic world and must piece together the events that led to the collapse of civilization.
40. In a world where nightmares are televised, a troubled teen confronts their own fears in dreams, emerging as an unexpected hero.
41. A teen gifted with time-rewinding abilities races against the clock to unravel a string of mysterious deaths and prevent an impending tragedy.
42. In a magical realm, a young mage-in-training embarks on a quest to unearth dark secrets from their mentor's past.
43. In a society of telepaths, one teen discovers their thoughts are impervious to intrusion, leading them on a journey to uncover their enigmatic origins.
44. When the seasons fall into chaos under the sway of magical entities, a teenager takes on the monumental task of restoring equilibrium.
45. Armed with the power to step into books, a teen becomes a literary detective, solving mysteries within the pages of classic novels.
46. In a world where memories are commodities, a young hero must reclaim stolen memories and reunite them with their rightful owners.
47. A talented young artist's prophetic sketches hold the key to averting impending disasters, forcing them into a role as an unlikely guardian.
48. Among floating islands in the sky, a winged teenager discovers a hidden civilization below the clouds, forever altering their destiny.
49. Endowed with the gift of healing, a reluctant teen hero emerges in the midst of a devastating plague outbreak.

50. In a world where people can communicate with animals, a teen must decipher a cryptic message from a group of endangered species.
51. A teen with the ability to control fire is chosen to protect a city threatened by volcanic eruptions.
52. In a future where memories can be erased, a teenager uncovers a government conspiracy to manipulate the past.
53. A young inventor builds a robot friend with unexpected abilities, leading to adventures and challenges.
54. In a world where everyone has a unique superpower, a teen with no apparent ability discovers their true strength.
55. A teenager with the power to bring drawings to life must navigate the consequences when their creations turn against them.
56. In a society divided by elemental powers, a teen with the ability to control multiple elements becomes a symbol of unity.
57. A group of teens discovers a hidden forest where mythical creatures exist, and they must protect it from those who seek to exploit its magic.
58. In a city where dreams are currency, a teen must navigate a dreamlike world to rescue their kidnapped sibling.
59. A young detective with a knack for solving puzzles investigates a series of art heists with cryptic clues left behind.
60. In a society where emotions are controlled through technology, a teen experiences a forbidden emotion and embarks on a journey to understand it.
61. A teenager with the power to see the past through objects must uncover a centuries-old mystery hidden in their town.
62. In a world where superheroes are real, a teen with a unique power must prove themselves among the heroes and villains.
63. A young warrior-in-training discovers a hidden academy for legendary heroes and sets out on a quest to prove their worth.
64. In a post-alien invasion world, a teen survivor must decode an extraterrestrial message that could save humanity.
65. A teenager in a magical kingdom becomes the guardian of a legendary artifact and must protect it from dark forces.
66. In a future where virtual reality has replaced reality, a teen hacker uncovers a sinister conspiracy within the virtual world.

67. A young scientist invents a device that allows time travel to historical events but accidentally alters the past, leading to unexpected consequences.
68. In a society where books are sentient, a teen forms a bond with a particular book that grants them special abilities.
69. A teenager with the power to understand and speak to animals embarks on a quest to save an endangered species.
70. In a post-apocalyptic wasteland, a group of teens discovers an ancient library and becomes the keepers of knowledge in a world without books.
71. A young alchemist discovers a hidden formula that grants the power of flight but attracts the attention of those who seek its destruction.
72. In a world where people can enter dreams, a teen with the ability to change dream outcomes becomes a dream detective.
73. A teenager with the power to control plants is tasked with restoring a dying forest to save their village.
74. In a society where colors have magical properties, a teen with the ability to manipulate color becomes a sought-after artist and protector.
75. A young linguist discovers an ancient language that holds the key to unlocking a hidden civilization.
76. In a future where music has been silenced, a teen musician must find a way to restore music to the world.
77. A teenager in a world of advanced technology finds a mysterious relic from the past and must uncover its significance.
78. In a city of shifting architecture, a teen with the ability to manipulate buildings becomes a hero and protector.
79. A young detective must solve a series of crimes involving stolen memories in a world where memories are bought and sold.
80. In a post-disaster world, a teen scientist creates a machine that can restore the environment but faces opposition from those who profit from the devastation.
81. A teenager with the power of telepathy forms a secret group to help others with their unique abilities.
82. In a magical academy, a student with no magical talent must uncover their hidden power to prevent a dark prophecy from coming true.

83. A young inventor builds a robot companion with artificial intelligence, and together they embark on a quest to uncover the inventor's family secrets.
84. In a future where dreams can be recorded, a teen with the ability to manipulate dreams becomes a sought-after artist and dream architect.
85. A teenager in a society of elemental magic must unite the elements to save their world from destruction.
86. In a world where wishes are granted but come at a cost, a teen must navigate a dangerous path of wishes and consequences.
87. A young archaeologist discovers an ancient artifact that allows them to communicate with civilizations from the past.
88. In a future where animals can talk, a teen forms an unlikely friendship with a wise old elephant and embarks on a journey to save endangered species.
89. A teenager with the power to control lightning becomes the protector of a city plagued by electrical storms.
90. In a world where everyone has a guardian spirit, a teen with a unique spirit must use their abilities to protect their community.
91. A young detective with a photographic memory is drawn into a web of conspiracies and must unravel the truth behind a series of unsolved mysteries.
92. In a post-apocalyptic world, a group of teens discovers a hidden bunker filled with advanced technology, sparking a battle for control.
93. A teenager with the ability to manipulate sound becomes a sought-after musician but must use their power to stop a sinister plot.
94. In a world where people can communicate with machines, a teen hacker must prevent a rogue AI from wreaking havoc.
95. A young mage-in-training discovers a forbidden spell that allows them to enter the pages of books and interact with their favorite fictional characters.
96. In a future where thoughts can be shared, a teenager with a unique ability to keep their thoughts private becomes a target of intrigue.
97. A teenager with the power to control ice must save their village from a never-ending winter caused by a powerful sorcerer.

98. In a society of shape-shifters, a teen with the ability to transform into any animal must unravel a mystery involving stolen identities.
99. A young artist discovers a magical paintbrush that brings their paintings to life but attracts the attention of art collectors and art thieves.
100. In a world where people can communicate with plants, a teenager must stop an invasive plant species from taking over the world.

14

Conclusion

As we stand at the crossroads of our literary odyssey through the vibrant world of storytelling, it's a moment that beckons us to pause and reflect on the magnificent journey we've undertaken together. Throughout these chapters, we've traversed diverse literary landscapes, peeling back the layers of the storytelling craft, and diving deep into the heart of creativity. With each genre we've explored, from the heart-pounding suspense of Thriller to the spine-tingling horrors of Horror, from the emotional crescendos of Romance to the visionary landscapes of Science Fiction, we've unearthed the essence of storytelling's limitless potential.

In our journey's beginning, we embarked on an exploration of the elusive Muse—the ethereal wellspring of inspiration that guides every writer's pen. We came to understand that the Muse isn't a tangible entity one can grasp, but rather a metaphorical representation of the boundless creativity residing within each of us. It's that inner force that whispers ideas, images, and emotions into our minds, fueling our innate desire to craft stories that resonate with the world.

Throughout this odyssey, one overarching truth has emerged, illuminated by the diverse genres we've encountered: storytelling knows no bounds. It is a canvas upon which we paint our dreams, fears, hopes, and aspirations. It's a tool for exploring the human condition, contemplating moral dilemmas, and sparking conversations about the world around us. Stories serve as bridges between cultures and generations, connecting us through shared experiences and universal themes.

In each chapter, we've uncovered the unique magic of every genre. We've learned that Adventure is more than epic quests; it's a metaphor for personal growth and transformation. Comedy isn't just about laughter; it's a reflection of our quirks and foibles. Crime stories aren't solely mysteries to solve; they dive into the complexities of morality and justice. Dystopian tales caution us about the consequences of our actions. Early Readers and Picture books are gateways to lifelong literacy.

Fantasy unleashes boundless creativity and invites us to believe in the extraordinary. Historical Fiction bridges the past and present, teaching us from history's lessons. Horror explores the darkest corners of the human psyche, while Mystery challenges our intellect. Romance captures the essence of human relationships and emotions, and Science Fiction propels us into speculative futures.

Each genre, with its unique charm, shares a common thread: storytelling's power to captivate, provoke thought, and inspire. As you, the storyteller, embrace these genres and their nuances, you embark on a profound journey of self-discovery. Your Muse, your source of inspiration, guides your storytelling path, leading you to weave narratives that leave indelible marks on your readers' hearts and minds.

Now, as you close this chapter of our collective storytelling voyage and prepare to face your own blank pages, remember that storytelling is both an art and an ongoing journey. It's about nurturing your creative spark, planting the seeds of ideas in the fertile soil of your imagination, and allowing them to grow into vibrant tales. It's about cultivating authenticity, emotion, and a touch of magic in your narratives, leaving your audience yearning for more.

Our exploration of the Muse of Story may be concluding here, but your storytelling journey has only just begun. If you've found inspiration within these pages, know that there are more treasures to uncover in "The Descriptors Handbook: Mastering Details in Your Writing" series. This series is a treasure trove of descriptors waiting to elevate your storytelling to new heights, much like we've explored the landscapes of genres, these books will guide you through the rich terrain of details. They're not just references; they are your keys to unlocking the intricacies of human features, the beauty of landscapes, and the architectural wonders that shape your stories.

"Mastering Human Features" dives into the subtleties of character descriptions, from facial expressions to body language and emotions. These descriptors breathe life into your characters, making them relatable, memorable, and multidimensional.

"Mastering Landscape Features" is your passport to crafting vivid, immersive settings, whether you're describing a lush forest, a bustling cityscape, or a desolate wasteland. This book equips you with the tools to paint landscapes that become characters in their own right.
And in "Mastering Architectural Features," you gain insights into the structures that define your story's world, from ancient castles to futuristic cities. These descriptors help you create environments that resonate with your readers.

As you continue your writing journey, remember that storytelling is an art of both grand narratives and exquisite details. By adding "The Descriptors Handbook" series to your toolkit, you'll possess the means to infuse your stories with richness and depth, inviting your readers to explore the intricacies of your worlds and characters.

Whether you're crafting epic adventures, heartwarming romances, or chilling mysteries, consider this series as your faithful companion, always ready to provide the perfect detail to make your stories truly extraordinary. With your imagination and these descriptors at your fingertips, your storytelling possibilities are as limitless as the Muse herself.

As you embark on this ongoing journey of storytelling mastery, may your creativity flow like a river, carrying your readers away into the boundless realms of your imagination. Your Muse is calling, and the worlds you create await your touch.

Other Titles

Mastering Human Features

Mastering Architectural Features

Mastering Landscape Features

www.ingramcontent.com/pod-product-compliance
Ingram Content Group UK Ltd.
Pitfield, Milton Keynes, MK11 3LW, UK
UKHW041445070726
13610UKWH00009B/22